Light and Heat

The Puritan View of the Pulpit

and

The Focus of the Gospel
in Puritan Preaching

by

Dr. R. Bruce Bickel

Soli Deo Gloria Publications
. . . for instruction in righteousness . . .

Soli Deo Gloria Publications
P.O. Box 451, Morgan, PA 15064
(412) 221-1901/FAX 221-1902

*

*

ISBN 1-57358-091-0

Contents

The Puritan View of the Pulpit

Preface   v

1. Introduction   1

2. The View of the Pulpit   7

3. The Direction of Preaching   14

     The Conviction of Preaching   14
     The Character of Preaching   22
     The Content of Preaching   30

4. The Demands of Preaching   38

5. The Duties of the Pastor   50

     Catechizing the People   54
     Counseling the Perplexed   57
     Comforting the Persecuted   61
     Communing in Private Worship   65

6. Conclusion   69

Bibliography   77

The Focus of the Gospel in Puritan Preaching

Preface   83

1. Introduction   85

2. The View of God   94

3. The View of Man   107

4. The View of the Person and Work of Christ   119

5. The View of Repentance and Faith   131

6. The View of Assurance   141

7. Conclusion   154

Bibliography   176

Appendix

A Comparative Overview of the Plan of Salvation   180

Preface

I have a deep concern for a paradox that exists within the evangelical community of our age. One may see a vigorous defense of the Word of God on one hand, but a low esteem for the preaching of that same Word as the means to build the church on the other. Many preachers today do not want to be considered "preachers," but rather "enablers" or "facilitators" of their flocks. With the increase of communication equipment and an emphasis on communication skills, Bible studies, small groups, and sharing are increasingly sought as the route to revitalizing the church, while faith in the pulpit fades and grows dim. Consequently, more emphasis is being placed on methodology and less on the message. I have therefore sought to go to a group of men who not only held a high view of the Word, but also held a high view of preaching that Word.

I have sought to read as many of the original works of the Puritans as possible while reserving the works *about* the Puritans to fill in the historical data not presented in their sermons or studies of divinity. Thus I have attempted to let the Puritan divines speak for themselves, and to reserve my observations for the conclusion. I also included three men whose ministry was shaped by their Puritan studies: Charles Spurgeon, Charles Bridges, and Martyn Lloyd-Jones. Although they did not minister in the historical Puritan period, their ministries were historically Puritan in direction and scope.

Dr. R. Bruce Bickel

The Puritan
View of the
Pulpit

Chapter 1

Introduction

Protestants, for the most part, have lost their confidence in one of the greatest assets of their tradition: the mysterious, creative power of the Word of God proclaimed from the pulpit. The desire to preach the Word in the pulpit has not endured in current evangelicalism because of the lost sense of the Word creating either situations or people who become doers of the Word. The picture of the one who preaches the Word from the pulpit as a doer of the Word appears to be dimming. This fading picture of the pulpit is a clear picture of how many Protestant ministers see their task and function. Their time is dictated by the vision they have of the pulpit. Many "share" rather than "preach," pray rather than pronounce blessings, and perform under a clouded vision of their ministry because they have no clear conviction about the nature of preaching. They do not see clearly the unique and supernatural nature of preaching because they do not see clearly the unique and supernatural nature of Holy Scripture.

Many ministers allocate their time accordingly. More time is spent in motivational discussions, program planning, and church administration than in sermon study and preparation. Both pastors and congregations alike organize the minister's schedule based on his or their view of the pulpit. Demands or expectations are placed upon the minister based upon a job description that reflects a weak view of the pulpit.

Throughout history, God has raised up men and movements whose great work was to preach and apply the Word of God to their own generation. Of course, by implication, these men have affected all generations thereafter—such men were the Puritans.

There has been much debate and confusion concerning the terms "Puritan" and "Puritanism." "Unfortunately, too often, rational, political, and social elements which were closely allied with the idea of Puritanism at various stages of its progress have largely obscured the vital religious and spiritual meaning of the term."[1] Without being exhaustive in defining these terms, one may say that Puritanism grew out of three central concepts: the New Testament pattern of personal piety, sound doctrine, and properly ordered church life.[2]

The blending of these elements made English Puritanism the astonishing movement that carried over into the New World in the first half of the eighteenth century. A brief understanding of these three elements will give us an account of the movement in history.

William Ames, an early leader in the movement, once defined divinity as "the doctrine of living to God." That definition describes the whole spirit of Puritanism. Peter Lewis states:

> Puritanism was not merely a set of rules or a larger creed, but a life-force: a vision and a compulsion which saw the beauty of a holy life and moved towards it, marvelling at the possibilities and thrilling to the satisfaction of a God-centered life. Moreover, iron discipline

---

[1] Peter Lewis. *The Genius of Puritanism* (Morgan, Pa.: Soli Deo Gloria, 1995), p. 11.
[2] *Ibid.*

was combined with fervent devotion, saving the Puritan from a fitful mysticism on the one hand, and a mere worldly religion on the other—and it was this marvelous marriage of law and grace which was not the least notable feature of Puritan piety. Every area of life came under the influence of God and the guidance of the Word.[3]

It was this "great business of Godliness" that dominated the Puritan's energies and ambitions and made the movement visible before men. Lewis summarizes the Puritan influence:

Men saw on earth lives that were not earthly, lives that touched their own at so many points, yet which rolled on into a moral and spiritual continent of breathtaking landscape.[4]

To the Puritan, piety did not grow out of the ground or materialize out of the air. Genuine godliness is the child of the royal marriage of truth with grace, and the godly Puritan was a child of both parents. There was of necessity a strong doctrinal belief that was the basis of their spiritual vitality. Lewis reveals the origin of such vitality:

Very Calvinistic in their theological tradition, they treasured a high conception of the sovereignty of God in providence and grace, and reflected this in tranquility with which they were able to carry themselves in the stormiest experiences and the forcefulness with which they were able to show the desperate needs and the unfailing resort of fallen man. If their doctrine of God

---

[3] *Ibid*, p. 12.
[4] *Ibid*.

elevated them, their doctrine of sin humbled them.[5]

In their books and sermons, the Puritan divines followed the devastating course of sin in all its guises, destroying self-confidence and directing men to that salvation which could be found only in the grace of God.

The third major tenet of Puritanism was the high position it gave to the doctrine of the Church. The vital questions that dominated the Puritan conscience could be summarized by the following: who rules the Church and the spiritual realm of life—God or man? Thus, these men began the ardent struggle to answer in practical terms whether the Church was to order her own course as distinct from the ruling monarch, and whether the Scriptures were to order the life of the Church distinct from ecclesiastical tradition. Citing Lewis again:

> The answer of the Puritans was a confident affirmative for the freedom of the Church under the sole sovereignty of the Scriptures.[6]

It was these three basic characteristics that formed the direction of the Puritan movement in history. The actual movement itself began around 1559 with the Act of Uniformity. In response to this attempt to make the English church more uniform in its ecclesiology, those who worked to purify and reform the church beyond what the government had established were called Puritans.[7] Lewis states that "it began under Elizabeth I who suspected it, grew under James I who

---

[5] *Ibid*, p. 13.

[6] *Ibid*, pp. 13-14.

[7] Tim Dowley, ed., *Eerdmans Handbook to the History of Christianity* (Grand Rapids: Eerdmans, 1978), p. 88.

feared it, increased in power under Charles I and his Arch-
bishop, William Laud, who despised it, gained a brief but
august ascendency under Cromwell who honored it, and
ended under Charles II and his bishops who hated it."[8]
Puritanism ended in its formal expression with the Act of
Uniformity of 1662. Although that may have been the date of
its official ending, the effects of Puritanism are to be found
far beyond the second half of the seventeenth century.

The Puritans soon found out that they were no match for
Elizabeth in the field of politics. Having been defeated po-
litically and having failed to reform the Church through par-
liamentary legislation, they began to reform the Church from
the bottom up by their vigorous persuasion from the pulpit,
the press, and their personal influence. This is the real story
of Puritanism. Concerning their impact, Lewis writes:

> From here on the real story of Puritanism is the story of
> its spiritual growth and power, and the history of the
> progress of Puritanism becomes not the record of
> councils and convocations, of legislation and counter-
> legislation, but the history of men whose crusade for a
> godly Church and a godly State could not be either
> much hindered or much helped by parliaments and their
> acts. Puritanism became a grass roots movement which
> the legislative scythe could limit but not destroy.[9]

Despite the persecution on the part of various monarchs
with the eventual exclusion of nearly 2000 of the Church's
best men before the winter of 1662, the question remains—
did all this achieve the destruction and failure of Puritanism?
Lewis powerfully answers:

---

[8] Lewis, p. 14.
[9] *Ibid*, pp. 14–15.

The answer of history stands: no, it did not. Puritanism, not destroyed but metamorphosed by persecution and political defeat, passed over into a thorough-going religious Non-conformity, and as such, began a new stage in its own and in the nation's religious development . . . a stage which survived to begin the notable period of missionary expansion that stretched from the Baptist, William Carey, in the 1790's to the massive missionary movements of Non-conformity in the Victorian era, a stage which survives in our own day in evangelical Non-conformity for which the lives and writings of the Puritan brotherhood stand as an abiding monument and an unquenched inspiration.[10]

---

[10] *Ibid*, p. 18.

Chapter 2

The View of the Pulpit

Puritan faith and Puritan life were closely bound together. Nowhere is this union better expressed than in the sermon literature of the period. As previously discussed, the real revolution generated by the Puritans was bloodless, spiritual and verbal. It was in the pulpit that they offered their greatest assault on the world's system, the flesh, and the devil. Describing the effects of their preaching, Lewis writes:

> From the despised "prophesyings" of Elizabeth's day to the hounded conventicles of Restoration England, the Puritan preaching was a power in the land. It was by turns tolerated, encouraged, and opposed; it was applauded, "refuted" and mocked; it was venerated and it was blasphemed—but it could not be, and never was ignored.[1]

Because the Puritans held that the pure Word of God was the criterion to which doctrine, worship, and church government must conform, proclamation of the Scriptures occupied the central position in their worship.

The importance of preaching consisted in the fact that it was the declaration by the preacher of the revelation of God, confirmed in the hearts of the believers by the interior

---

[1] Peter Lewis, *The Genius of Puritanism* (Morgan, Pa.: Soli Deo Gloria, 1995) p. 19.

The Puritan View of the Pulpit

8

testimony of the Holy Spirit.[2]

For the Puritan, who emphasized the great abyss that separated God from man, his view of the pulpit was derived from his high view of God. Thomas Watson said concerning the one God:

> If a ship should have two pilots of equal power, one would be ever crossing the other; when one would sail, the other would cast anchor; here were a confusion, and the ship must needs perish. The order and harmony in the world, the constant and uniform government of all things, is a clear argument that there is but one Omnipotent, one God that rules all.[3]

Watson again said, "God's center is everywhere, His circumference nowhere."[4] And "God can make a straight stroke with a crooked stick."[5]

The urbane and polished, yet cosmopolitan Richard Sibbes wrote, "How could finite comprehend infinite? We shall apprehend Him, but not comprehend Him."[6]

The lesser known Christopher Nesse said, concerning the sovereign God, "God is the cause of causes."[7]

Their high view of God made it infinitely more important that God should cross the separation-gap and speak to them through the sermon than that they should travel across it in prayer or praise. Richard Baxter gave perhaps the finest

---

[2] Horton Davies, *The Worship of the English Puritans* (Morgan, Pa:. Soli Deo Gloria, 1997), p. 182.
[3] I. D. E. Thomas, comp. ed., *The Golden Treasury of Puritan Quotations* (Carlisle: Banner of Truth, 1977), p. 117.
[4] *Ibid*, p. 119
[5] *Ibid*.
[6] *Ibid*, p. 118.
[7] *Ibid*, p. 119.

definition of the purpose and position of preaching expressed by the Puritans.

> It is no small matter to stand up in the face of a congregation, and deliver a message of salvation or damnation, as from the living God, in the name of our Redeemer. It is no easy matter to speak so plain, that the ignorant may understand us; and so seriously that the deadest hearts may feel us; and so convincingly, that contradicting cavillers may be silenced.[8]

For a true appreciation of their view of the pulpit and its being defined by a sovereign and holy God, it is necessary to turn to more leading Puritan authors. One of the earliest, William Bradshaw, claimed to speak for the whole body of Puritans as indicated by this excerpt from one of his works:

> They hold that the highest and supreme office and authority of the Pastor, is to preach the gospel solemnly and publicly to the Congregation, by interpreting the written word of God, and applying the same by exhortation and reproof unto them. They hold that this was the greatest work that Christ and his apostles did.[9]

Arthur Hildersham expounded and applied this observation concerning the work of Christ when he wrote:

> Preaching was the chief work of all that Christ, the chief pastor, was sent to do in his ministry. Luke 4:18, 43 . . . neither was there any one work of his calling that he did so much and so diligently exercise himself in as in preaching. . . . Christ sent me, saith the apostle, I

---

[8] Richard Baxter, *The Reformed Pastor*, ed. William Brown (5th ed. 1656; rpt. Carlisle, Pa.: Banner of Truth, 1979), p. 128.
[9] Davies, p. 183.

Cor. 1:17, not to baptise (that is not so much to
baptise) but to preach the gospel . . . and this is the
chief work that we are called to exercise ourselves in . . .
gladly taking all opportunities for doing this work.[10]

Henry Smith was perhaps the orator par excellence of the
movement. He spoke concerning preaching:

Christ asked his disciples what they thought of him,
Matt. 16:13, so I would ask you, what do you think of
preachers? Is he a contemptible person which bringeth
the message of God; which hath the name of an Angel
(2 Cor. 5:20), and all his words are messages of life?
Prophets are of such account with God, that it is said,
Amos 3:7: God will do nothing before he reveals it unto
his prophets; so prophets are, as it were, God's counsel-
lors.[11]

One can note clearly the progression that begins with
God giving the ministry of preaching to His Son, the Son
giving the ministry to His apostles, and thence to all ministers of the gospel. Another Puritan, Paul Bayne, showed this
line of thinking when he examined Paul's letter to the
Ephesians, a church which our Lord never visited in person
while on earth:

And he came and preached peace to you who were far
off and peace to those who were near, Eph. 2:17: He
saith Christ preached to them. . . . Now he was never a
minister but of the circumcism (Rom. 15:8), to the lost
sheep of the house of Israel (Matt. 15:24) in his person.
Therefore we see that Christ is present and hath a part
in preaching even when men preach ("you seek a proof

---

[10] Lewis, p. 35.
[11] *Ibid*, pp. 34-35.

> of Christ speaking in me", 2 Cor. 13:3) . . . for this is
> the office of Christ our great Prophet, not only in his
> own person to open to us the will of the Father . . . but
> to be present and teach inwardly in the heart with that
> Word which is outwardly sounded unto the ear by men
> . . . Thus Paul preached to the ear, but Christ to the
> heart of Lydia. This must teach us to look upon Christ
> as the Chief Prophet among us, and the chief Preacher
> whosoever speaketh.[12]

These great men of faith took seriously the mysterious
words of Jesus, "He who hears you hears Me" (Luke 10:16).
In the sober light of these words, the Puritans enthusiasti-
cally elevated the preaching office to a position reminiscent
of apostolic times. Richard Sibbes spoke for all Puritan
preachers when he said:

> Christ, when he ascended on high and led captivity
> captive (he would give no mean gift then, when he was
> to ascend triumphantly to heaven) the greatest he could
> give was "some to be prophets, some apostles, some
> teachers (and preachers) for the building up of the body
> of Christ till we all meet, a perfect man in Christ." "I
> will send them pastors according to my own heart,"
> saith God (Jer. 3:15). It is the gift of all gifts, the ordi-
> nance of preaching. God esteems it so, Christ esteems
> it so, and so should we esteem it.[13]

Another manner in which to observe the high value of
the pulpit is to examine the debate between the Anglicans
and the Puritans on the relative merits of homilies and sermons. This issue will be examined more fully in Chapter 3,

---

[12] *Ibid*, p. 36.

[13] Richard Sibbes, *The Works of Richard Sibbes*, ed. Alexander B. Grosart,
(2nd ed. 1862-64; rpt. Carlisle, Pa.: Banner of Truth, 1978), V:462.

but it does indeed demonstrate the indispensable value which the Puritans attached to the pulpit. The pulpit was God's appointed means of bringing men to salvation and also served as the best means of gaining the interest of a congregation and of educating it. Moreover, they believed strongly that only sermons, and not readings, could adapt themselves to the needs of a particular group of people. Thomas Watson wrote:

> It was by the ear, by our first parents listening to the serpent, that we lost paradise; and it is by the ear, by hearing of the Word preached, that we get to heaven. "Hear, and your souls shall live" (Isaiah 55:3).[14]

Consequently, they made the exposition and discussion of the Scriptures the outstanding feature in their worship. Their reverence for the Bible as the only standard for worship produced the Puritan appreciation of the sermon as the culminating point of the worship of God. "For them the obedient listening to the exposition of the sacred oracles of God was the climax of the service."[15]

The Puritan preachers' humble dignity in their high and holy office is seen in what is not recorded in the titles of most of their books. One is hard pressed to find, for instance, any record of academic distinction after the name of Thomas Brooks. Brooks, like most other Puritans, places nothing on the title page except the more nobler designation "Preacher of the Word" or "Preacher of the Gospel."

Their high view of God was described by Stephen Charnock: "It is a less wrong to God to discard any acknowl-

---

[14] Thomas, p. 221.
[15] Davies, p. 188.

edgments of his being, and to count him nothing, than to believe him to exist, but to imagine a base and unholy Diety; he that saith, God is not holy, speaks much worse than he that saith, There is no God at all."[16] Thus, wherever Puritanism was strong, its concept of the pulpit was very evident. As a result the office of preacher and teacher was elevated to a place of dignity and prominence. Lewis states the derivation of such dignity:

> Godward, preaching derived its honor from the seal which God had placed upon it by which it was endowed with particular spiritual potency for the conversion of men and their building up in the faith; manward, its dignity was increased by the human need for it, to inspire, instruct, warn, rebuke, and comfort.[17]

This high view of God and His subsequent appointment of men to be preachers of the gospel message, the means by which the God of holy love chose to win and save souls, determined the aim of their entire ministry. To the Puritan minister, his principal duty was to preach. To them, the end of that ministry was to be judged in light of its aim. That aim was the glory of God and the persuasion of each man to live a life submitted absolutely to the will of God. To this end their sermons were directed with unrestrained passion. Everything in their lives and service was to make tribute to this glorious purpose and lofty ideal. Their entire life and ministry was shaped by their view of the pulpit.

---

[16] Stephen Charnock, *Discourses Upon the Existence and Attributes of God* (3rd ed.; Grand Rapids: Baker Book House, 1981), p. 113.
[17] Lewis, p. 37.

Chapter 3

The Direction of Preaching

The Conviction of Preaching

In October 1682, near the evening of the Puritan age, Robert Traill delivered a sermon in continuation of morning exercises held by the Puritans in or near London. The sermon was entitled "By What Means May Ministers Best Win Souls?" Traill expressed the conviction of all Puritan preachers when he said, "The principal work of a minister is preaching; the principal benefit people have by them is to hear the Lord's word from them."[1]

Traill almost repeated the words spoken by William Perkins at the early dawning of the Puritan age.[2] To this end countless men gave themselves in packed Parliaments, crowded cellars of private homes or open fields in the early morning hours. To the Puritans, an unpreaching minister was a sort of contradiction.

When one reads such statements as those written by Thomas Brooks in his exposition on the riches of Christ, it is easily understood why these men elevated the role of preaching as their chief duty. He answers the question "Why is it the great work and duty of ministers to preach Jesus Christ to the people?" with the following observations:

---

[1] Robert Traill, "By What Means May Ministers Best Win Souls?" in *Puritan Sermons: 1659-1689*, translator James Nichols (Wheaton: Richard Owen Roberts, 1981), III:207, hereafter referred to as *Puritan Sermons*.
[2] Peter Lewis, *The Genius of Puritanism* (Morgan, Pa.: Soli Deo Gloria, 1995), p. 37.

Thomas Goodwin, *The Works of Thomas Goodwin* (rpt. Louisville, Miss.; Morton Davis Publishing, 1979), XI:360–361.

> First, because that is the only way to save and to win
> souls to Jesus Christ. . . . Secondly, they are to preach
> Christ to the people because it is the choicest and
> chiefest way to ingratiate Christ with poor souls. . . .
> Thirdly, it is their chief duty to preach Jesus Christ to
> the people because the preaching up of Christ is the
> only way to preach down antichrist, or whatever else
> makes against Christ. Fourthly, is this, because else they
> contract upon themselves the blood of souls. . . . The
> last reason because the preaching of Christ contributes
> most to their comfort here, and to their reward here-
> after; therefore, they are to preach the Lord Christ to
> people.[3]

John Downame's statement that preaching is "God's own
ordinance which he hath instituted and ordained for the
gathering of the saints, and the building of his Church, as ap-
peareth by Eph. 4:11–12,"[4] was representative of the Puritan
mindset. By this they did not mean that preaching was the
exclusive means of saving men, but it was considered to be
God's *principal* means of gathering His Church.

Thomas White delivered an early morning lecture in the
Cripplegate Exercises and expressed this universal mandate
of the Puritan movement:

> The most ordinary means of our effectual calling is the
> preaching of the Word . . . and though by other means
> men may be called, yet seldom or never any are called
> that neglect and condemn this.[5]

---

[3] Thomas Brooks, *The Works of Thomas Brooks*, ed. Alexander B. Grosart
(1862-64; rpt. Carlisle, Pa.: Banner of Truth, 1980), III:207–210.
[4] Lewis, p. 39.
[5] *Puritan Sermons*, V: 278.

The statement of Thomas Goodwin is perhaps the clearest illustration of their deep conviction that the gospel is the
power of God unto salvation (Rom. 1:16; 1 Cor. 1:21; Jas.
1:18) when it is preached—not sung, danced, or acted:

> 1. It is so appointed and ordained by God (Isa. 55:10–11)
> 2. As God appointed it, so Christ prayed for it (John
> 17:19–20)
> 3. As God the Father appointed it, and God the Son
> prayed for it, so God the Holy Spirit is, by promise and
> covenant engaged to accompany it with his blessing
> unto the seed of Christ forever (Isa. 59:21)[6]

It is interesting to compare the debate between the
Anglicans and the Puritans on the merits of the sermon with
other more established avenues that were thought to lead to a
saving knowledge of God. Granted, there may have been
some warrant on the part of the Establishment for their fear
that the Puritans would use the sermon as a means to dissem-
inate some of their distinctive political tenets; nevertheless,
the debate went much deeper than mere political ideologies.
The Establishment saw "conversation in the bosom of the
church, religious education, the reading of learned men's
books, information received by conference, as well as the
public and private reading of the Scriptures and of homilies
as other avenues that lead to a saving knowledge of God."[7]
Thus, in the eyes of many, the value which the Puritans
placed on the sermon was excessive. Homilies, discourses on
certain subjects, were preferred to sermons because they

---

[6] Thomas Goodwin, *The Works of Thomas Goodwin* (rpt. Louisville,
Miss.; Mounts Publishing, 1979), XI:360–361.
[7] Horton Davies, *The Worship of the English Puritans* (Morgan, Pa.: Soli
Deo Gloria), p. 185.

were more carefully prepared, the Anglicans said. Sermons were thought to be the corrupt productions of men while the reading of the Scripture preserved the Word of God unadulterated.[8]

The Puritans took a different view of the preaching of sermons. While they recognized that reading may make one wise unto salvation, readings were a poor substitute for preaching because preaching alone was how the Word of God would penetrate the hearts of the congregation. Thomas Cartwright responded to these allegations: "As the fire stirred giveth more heat, so the Word, as it were, blown by preaching, flameth more in the hearers, than when it is read."[9]

The main complaint that the Puritans had against Anglican sermons was that they were not evangelical in content. The Anglican Church during the Puritan era produced many eloquent preachers, but they were recognized primarily as orators rather than preachers. The difference in the Anglican concept of the sermon stemmed from their view of the pulpit. One Puritan writer described Anglican sermons as "orations of the excellent Constitution of their Church, or of Passive Obedience, or an Exclamation against Schism, or a Discourse of Morality, or only exclaiming against such vices as the very light of Nature condemns.' "[10] In contrast, Richard Baxter provided the classical description of the urgency of preaching as "a dying man to dying men."[11]

---

[8] *Ibid*, p. 186.
[9] *Ibid*.
[10] *Ibid*, p. 202.
[11] I.D.E. Thomas, comp. ed., *The Golden Treasury of Puritan Quotations* (Carlisle, Pa.: Banner of Truth, 1977), p. 223.

Basically, the Puritan charge against the Anglicans was the lack of earnestness in the Establishment. For the Puritan, a true zeal for conversion was discernible only in a minister who preached the evangelical doctrines with vigor. Davies captures their intensity:

> The Puritan's concern was light and heat. The Anglican despised enthusiasm in the pulpit, and in his zeal to be the servant of the State occasionally forgot that he was the servant of God. But the Puritan preacher, whose dominating desire was to win souls, and who supplemented his preaching with diligent visitation, determined like St. Paul, "to know nothing save Jesus Christ and him crucified." To this aim all was directed.[12]

Baxter stated the urgency of preaching in another way:

> Let the awful and important thoughts of souls being saved by my preaching, or left to perish and be condemned to hell by my negligency, I say, let this awful and tremendous thought dwell ever upon your spirit.[13]

The above quotations significantly illustrate the Puritan conviction of the importance of the sermon. They believed that the preacher was the man of God, the prophet, who declared to the people the gospel mystery. They saw themselves, because of their view of the pulpit, as the ones who were required to unfold the whole plan of salvation. What might have appeared as mere enthusiasm in the Puritan preacher was in reality an expression of his sense of urgency. To these men, they were actually under the authority of Christ binding and loosing the souls of men. To the Puritan

---

[12] Davies, p. 202.
[13] *Ibid*, pp. 184–185.

pastor, the preaching of the Word of God was not a moral homily or a philosophical discourse; it was the authoritative proclamation of the will of the blessed, holy God. How they saw God determined how they saw themselves in their pulpits. They viewed themselves as men sovereignly appointed by God to declare a message that was not their own, but a message that had already been given by God Himself in the pages of sacred writ.

Under such conviction, no wonder "a Puritan preacher mounted the steps of his pulpit as if he were a Moses ascending the mountain of Sinai."[14]

In response to the accusations by the Anglicans that the Puritans put too much emphasis on their preaching, one only has to let devout Thomas Goodwin speak:

> It is not the letter of the Word that ordinarily doth convert, but the spiritual meaning of it, as revealed and expounded. . . . There is the letter, the husk; and there is the spirit, the kernel; and when we by expounding the word do open the husk, out drops the kernel. And so it is the spiritual meaning of the Word let into the heart which converts it and turns it unto God.[15]

Goodwin also added somewhat humorously in the same sermon that the very dullness of many people necessitated the act of preaching the Scriptures.

Another indication of the depth of the Puritan conviction of preaching can be observed in the frequency of the demand for preaching. In his diary, Richard Baxter provides an indication of his ministerial labors: "I preached before the Wars twice each Lord's Day; but after the War but once, and once

---

14 *Ibid*, p. 184.
15 Goodwin, II:361.

every Thursday, besides occasional sermons."[16]

It must be added that this did not make up all his pastoral duties, for he spent two days a week in catechizing families. This extension of the ministry of the pulpit will be developed more fully in the following chapter.

Even more profound is a remarkable example taken from the diary of Oliver Heywood, who in reviewing his efforts in the year 1689, when he had reached the age of sixty, declared: "I doe find that I had travelled 1358 miles, preacht 131 times in weekdays, kept 34 fasts, 8 days of thanksgiving, baptized 21 children . . ."[17] Davies underscores this illustration:

> The following year he records that he has preached 135 times in week-days including two sermons every Lord's day. This Puritan pastor preached, on an average, five sermons per week. He was not an itinerant preacher, attached to no church. He was the minister of the church of Northwram, near Halifax. He was an author of great merit in his day. His many sermons were, therefore, preached in the midst of an unusually busy life.[18]

One hardly could hope to find a more vivid example of the deep sense of conviction that the Puritans had of their calling as preachers of the Word.

The Puritan conviction for preaching did not isolate itself to the lost. On the contrary, Richard Sibbes stated:

> The Word of God preached . . . is not altogether to teach us, but that the Spirit going with it might work grace necessary to strengthen us in the inward man.

---

16 Davies, p. 202.
17 *Ibid*, p. 201.
18 *Ibid*.

> 2 Cor. 4:16 . . . Let us therefore set a price upon God's
> ordinance. There must be this dispensation.[19]

The vital necessity of preaching the Word of God, as
distinct from mere reading, is stated clearly by John Owen:

> The word is like the sun in the firmament. Thereunto
> it is compared at large. Ps. 19. It hath virtually in it all
> spiritual light and heat. But the preaching of the word is
> as the motion and beams of the sun, which actually and
> effectually communicate that light and heat unto all
> creatures, which are virtually (essentially and energeti-
> cally) in the sun itself.[20]

Nehemiah Rogers concluded that "The text is the word
of God abridged; preaching is the word of God enlarged."[21]

To the Puritans, the conviction of their preaching was "to
save the sinner and edify the saint." That statement made by
Horatius Bonar a century later clearly indicates the impact of
the Puritan mindset on some of the great preachers of later
generations.

In reflecting on the conviction that their preaching was
critical for the building up of the saints, Lewis quotes
Nicholas Byfield, and thoroughly summarizes the good that
comes to men through the preaching of the whole council of
God. He records:

> What good shall men get by hearing of sermons? Many
> are the singular benefits that come to men thereby.

---

[19] Richard Sibbes, *The Works of Richard Sibbes*, ed. Alexander B. Grosart,
(2nd. ed.; 1862–64; rpt. Carlisle, Pa.: Banner of Truth, 1978), V:508.
[20] John Owen, *The Works of John Owen*, ed. William H. Goold, (3rd. ed.
1850–53; Carlisle, Pa.: Banner of Truth, 1977), VI:245.
[21] Thomas, p. 222.

First, the Holy Ghost is here given, Acts 10:44.
Secondly, men's hearts are here opened, Acts 16:14.
Thirdly, the fear of God doth here fall upon men, Acts
13:16. Fourthly, the proud and stony heart of men is
here tamed, melted, and made to tremble, Is. 66:2.
Fifthly, the faith of God's elect is here begotten, Rom.
10:14. Sixthly, men are here sealed by the Holy Spirit
of promise, Eph. 1:13. Seventhly, here the Spirit
speaketh to the churches, Eph. 1:13. Eighthly, Christ
here comes to sup with men, Rev. 3:20, let men tell of
their experience, whether ever their hearts tasted of
the refreshing of Christ till they devoted themselves to
the hearing of the Word. Ninthly, the painful distress
of the afflicted conscience is here or nowhere cured by
hearing, the bones that God hath broken receive joy and
gladness, Ps. 51:8. Tenthly, what shall I say, but as the
Evangelical Prophet saith? "If you can do nothing else,
yet hear, and your soul shall live," Is. 55:3. Live, I say,
the life of grace, yea, and the life of glory: for salvation
is brought to us by hearing, Acts 28:28.[22]

Having seen God clearly in His Word, the Puritans elevated and defended the conviction of the preaching ministry not on the grounds of personal interest, but on the deep aim of glorifying God "through the Church that then was, and the Church that was yet to be."[23]

The Character of Preaching

The sermon was the Puritan minister's attempt through reason to encourage faith as it affected this life and the next. They were committed to a style that was plain, but not dull. Each minister was pledged by his own creed to use a balance of doctrine and practice, faithfully devoted to the exposition

---

22 Lewis, pp. 42–43.
23 *Ibid.*

of the Word of Scripture, and understood by all. In this golden era of great expositors, nothing is more striking than to read the great thought poured into their plain and practical preaching. Even the early textbooks used at Harvard and Yale until the middle of the eighteenth century reflected and defended this Puritan tenet of preaching. Perry Miller has elucidated this period in a discussion of "The Plain Style":

> The doctrines of the organization of the sermon and of the plain style were prominent in the intellectual inheritance of the New Englanders. By them was determined the form and technique of the sermon, of the one literary type in which the Puritan spirit was most completely expressed.[24]

The character of the Puritan sermon contained a deep conviction that the nature of the sermon should be practical. This deep conviction was evidenced by John Flavel:

> A crucified style best suits the preachers of a crucified Christ. . . . Prudence will choose words that are solid, rather than florid: as a merchant will choose a ship by a sound bottom, and capacious hold, rather than a gilded head and stern. Words are but servants to matter. An iron key, fitted to the wards of the lock, is more useful than a golden one that will not open the door to the treasures. . . . Prudence will cast away a thousand fine words for one that is apt to penetrate the conscience and reach the heart.[25]

Lewis quotes Richard Baxter, perhaps the master of plain

---

[24] Perry Miller, *The New England Mind* (Boston: Beacon Press, 1961), p. 336.
[25] John Flavel, *The Works of John Flavel* (2nd. ed.; 1820; Carlisle, Pa.: Banner of Truth, 1982), VI:568.

yet potent preaching, as logically stating: "If you would not
teach men, what do you in the pulpit?"[26] To that end, the
Puritan preacher "employed every lawful aid of native wit
and acquired art; anecdote and allegory; metaphor and sim-
ile, to help gain the attention and to win the hearts and lives
of their hearers for their divine Master."[27]

Jonathan Edwards was greatly influenced by the works of
William Ames, who instructed his students thus:

> Preaching therefore ought not to be dead, but lively and
> effectuall, so that an unbeliever coming into the Con-
> gregation of the faithful he ought to be affected, and as
> it were digged through with the very hearing of the
> Word, that he may give glory to God.[28]

The character of the Puritan sermon was such that it had
enough rhetoric to get through to the heart, but never so
much that the understanding of the simple or the earnest was
hindered.

Every Puritan sermon began with a definite biblical text.
Once a text was selected, the preacher's immediate duty was
to clarify it in all possible ways. Thus, the lengthy Puritan
sermon has a structure of its own. Basically, it had a triple
division: Doctrine, Reason, and Use.[29] In contrast to the
sermons of the Anglican divines, such as Lancelot Andrewes
and John Donne (which sermons were weighed down with
classical quotations), the sermons of the Puritans were re-
stricted almost entirely to biblical citations, because evan-

---

[26] Lewis, p. 48.

[27] *Ibid.*

[28] Ralph Turnbull, *Jonathan Edwards: The Preacher* (Grand Rapids:
Baker Book House, 1958), p. 52.

[29] Davies, p. 191.

gelical teaching was the first aim of the sermon. Each sermon was an attempt to identify from the text an axiom of theology, and to discuss its practical applications. In procedure, the text was taken apart by the method of analysis into its component parts and usually set out again as a proposition. After the logical analysis of the passage, the practical appeal was made by the pastor-teacher, who attempted to make the Bible applicable to real life. In defining the process, Davies observes:

> The doctrines had to be explained to the congregation and their contraries refuted. The second division of the sermon was a logical defence of the assumptions of the first section. It was insisted that apparent contradictions were to be reconciled, and that little time was to be spent in answering trivial objections or mere cavillings. The third section was intended to drive home the practical advantages of belief in the particular teachings advocated. It usually concluded with admonitions and encouragements.[30]

Perhaps another way of structuring the Puritan sermon would be the Declaration, the Explanation, and the Application. The first two divisions were to convince the reason, while the last division was aimed at warming the heart's affections into accepting the doctrine of the first division.

Davies affirms this tradition among the Puritans by quoting Baxter:

> The preacher's aim should be first to convince the understanding and then to engage the heart. Light first, then heat. Begin with a careful opening of the text, then proceed to the clearance of possible difficulties or

---

30 *Ibid.*

> objections; next, to a statement of uses; and lastly to a
> fervent appeal for acceptance by conscience and heart.[31]

The Puritans preached lengthy sermons and adhered to a method of structure with unfailing regularity. Their divisions were named, the points under each one were numbered, and the objections were presented and answered in order. The sermons were examples of thoroughly reasoned theological thinking with searching application in practical insights into life. Yet while being masters of divinity, they were also masters of practical divinity. To these men of the Word, there was no doctrine that could not be practiced; to them, all that was practiced had to be founded on sound doctrine.

One only needs to read the wealth of Puritan literature that has recently been reprinted to observe their patterns of preparation and the character of their preaching. An observation from the work of Issac Watts will, however, describe the perfect Puritan sermon. Davies cites Watts as stating:

> Awaken your spirit, therefore, in your composures, contrive all lively, forcible and penetrating form of speech, to make your words powerful and impressive on the hearts of your hearers, when light is first let into the mind. . . . Practice the awful and solemn ways of address to the conscience, all the soft and tender influences on the heart. Try all methods to rouse and awaken the cold, the stupid, the sleepy race of sinners; learn all the language of holy jealousy and terror, to affright the presumptions; all the compassionate and encouraging manners of speaking, to comfort, encourage, and direct the awakened, the penitent, the willing, and the humble; all the winning and engaging modes of discourse and expos-

---

[31] *Ibid*, p. 192.

tulation, to constrain the hearers of every character to attend. Seek this happy skill of reigning and triumphing over the hearts of an assembly; persuade them with power to love and practice all the important duties of godliness, in oppostion to the flesh and the world; endeavour to kindle the soul to zeal in the holy warfare, and to make it bravely victorious over all the enemies of its salvation.[32]

The structure of the Puritan sermon was designed to reach these lofty ideals, and often the preachers would use "vehement gestures in the delivery of their sermons."[33] Phraseology was another characteristic of the sermon that brought both approval from their own congregations and abomination from the Anglicans. In their minds, however, the Puritans considered themselves to have apostolic precedents in using such terms as "God's saints," "the Lord's holy ones," "the dear people of God," "the little flock," "the lambs of Jesus Christ," "the Redeemed of Zion," or "the precious, elect seed." The Puritans deeply loved their flocks, so it is probably more fair to assume that their distinctive biblical phraseology was due to love and familiarity with the Scriptures, not to exhibition.

The sermons themselves offer clear evidence that the Puritan preacher carefully prepared them for the edification of the people. Because these preachers affirmed that the chief end of preaching was "the glorification of God in the restoration of his image in the souls and lives of men,"[34] their great desire was to see their preaching result in practice.

---

[32] *Ibid.*
[33] *Ibid*, p. 194.
[34] Lewis, p. 48.

If Puritan preaching was plain, it was also highly practical. No matter what point of faith or behavior they wished to establish, they clarified it by sermonic similitudes, especially by suggesting comparisons. Because they saw the physical world through the eyes of the Bible, they had a wealth of comparisons to make in illustrating their desired responses.

Generally, a Puritan preacher would make application of the desired doctrine as follows: The congregation would be asked to recall some fact or incident that by normal observation they knew to be true. Then they were asked to apply to their faith the practical truth they had just recognized as common knowledge. Thus, when the preacher needed to confirm the greatness of Christ, he would speak in terms of kings. Wouldn't an ordinary man make great preparations for the visit of a king? Wouldn't he humbly beg for his favors? Could anyone, then, do less for the King of kings? In reading Puritan sermons, one will find varied references to birds, butterflies, storms, mariners, nautical images, mountains, valleys, and a vast array of everyday life examples, all designed to facilitate the application of the doctrine stated.

With this high emphasis on edification and application, the authors of the Puritan sermons made every effort to make the sermons as easy to remember as possible. One particular method that was widely used was to begin the heading of each division or doctrine of the sermon with the same letter. They contended that this method would make for easy retention in the memory. Davies selects one of a myriad of examples from a sermon by Richard Baxter as an illustration:

> As if I were to direct you to the chiefest helps to your salvation, and should name, 1. Powerful Preaching, 2.

Prayer, 3. Prudence, 4. Piety, 5. Painfulness, 6. Patience, 7. Perseverance.[35]

In reflecting upon the influence of this plain style and its variations upon the early New England preacher, Babette Levy writes:

> The natural variations in ability are, then, apparent in the preaching of New England's first pastors. All had the Biblical and theological culture peculiar to seventeenth-century Puritanism. All these ministers were equally earnest in their effort to convince of the necessity for faith and to admonish the various sinners inevitably in any gathering, even of the elect. Simplicity of pulpit style was deliberately cultivated, but purposeful sincerity seems to have been instinctive with New England's first ministers, who managed—as few men have managed—to forget themselves in Christ's cause.[36]

Puritanism was a way of life as well as a manner of thought. Puritan preaching was aimed, therefore, not only at informing the understanding, but also at influencing the will and reforming the life. Here, in summary, is the character of the preaching ministry as stated by Jonathan Edwards:

> As the servant of the Word the pastor's message out of the Word should cleanse the consciences of the people who listen to him. The whole church is edified and built up by this soul-washing, hence the primary importance of the pastor is to be an expository preacher.[37]

---

[35] Davies, p. 196.
[36] Babette M. Levy, *Preaching in the First Half Century of New England History* (New York: Russell & Russell, 1944), pp. 155–156.
[37] Turnbull, p. 114.

The Content of Preaching

The Puritan's concern was light and heat—light from the pure Word of God to penetrate the darkness of the heart and soul of the hearer, heat from the pathos and passion of the heart and soul of the preacher to bring about conviction. The main work of the gospel minister, according to the Puritans, was to preach the saving efficacy of the redeeming work of the holy Sovereign. Christ was seen as the end of the law for righteousness. Thus, for sinful man to find acceptance with a holy and righteous God, grace must intervene in history and in life. From their study of the New Testament, and their understanding of God's defined pulpit responsibilities given to them as ministers of the Word, they placed the emphasis on grace—the summation of the matchless love of God's holy nature—and pressed it on to others.

The Puritan preachers were men who believed profoundly in preaching grace. To these expositors, the sermon was an agency of redemption. The content of their sermons was a result of grace in their own hearts. The Puritan could never get away from the wonder and glory of his own spiritual illumination. While others might stress the sacraments as a converting means in a day of religious formalism, the Puritans restored the sermon to its primacy and focal point of worship. The content of their sermons, to both sinner and saint, was the doctrine of grace. The realization of God's sovereign grace in their own lives inspired them to magnify the grace of God when they preached, and to seek the conversion of others.

The content of Puritan preaching was the consistent expression of their conviction that the conversion of a sinner was a gracious sovereign work of Divine power; thus, they preached that all self-effort or resolve would be vain unless grace actively operated to assist. The conversion of evangelist George Whitefield reveals not only the Puritans' understanding of salvation, but also a picture of the glorious experience that motivated these men to preach the gospel. In discussing Whitefield's conversion, Arnold Dallimore writes:

> But now, when he had come to an end of all human resources, when there was nothing else that he could do to seek salvation, God revealed Himself in grace, and granted him that which he had found could never be earned. Somehow, we know not exactly how: somewhere, perhaps in his room, or more likely, in one of the secluded Oxford walks, in a sense of utter desperation, in rejection of all self-trust, he cast his soul on the mercy of God through Jesus Christ, and a ray of faith, granted him from above, assured him he would not be cast out.[38]

Then he recalls Whitefield's testimony of this experience:

> God was pleased to remove the heavy load, to enable me to lay hold of His dear Son by a living faith, and by giving me the Spirit of adoption, to seal me even to the day of everlasting redemption. O! with what joy—joy unspeakable—even joy that was full of and big with glory, was my soul filled, when the weight of sin went off, and an abiding sense of the pardoning love of God, and a full assurance of faith, broke in upon my disconsolate soul! Surely it was the day of mine espousals—a day to be had in everlasting remembrance! At first my joys were like a spring tide, and overflowed the banks.[39]

---

[38] Arnold A. Dallimore, *George Whitefield* (Westchester, Il.: Cornerstone Books, 1979), I:77.
[39] *Ibid.*

These statements reveal certain fundamental truths about the message delivered by the Puritans: they knew that salvation was a Divine work—the placing of the life of God in the soul of man—and that it was an external work. It also reveals that the Puritan message centered on the doctrines of grace, or the system known as Calvinism.

Thomas Watson, in a reference to God's effectual call through the preaching of the Word and the ministry of the Holy Spirit, said, "Ministers knock at the door of men's hearts, the Spirit comes with a key and opens the door."[40]

While our purpose is not to compare the teachings of Calvinism on grace with the hypothesis of Arminian grace, it must be stated that the reason why the Puritans thus magnified the quickening power of God in preaching was that "they took so seriously the Bible teaching that man is dead in sin, radically depraved, sin's helpless bondslave. There is, they held, such a strength in sin that only Omnipotence can break its bond; and only the Author of life can raise the dead."[41] The Puritans taught total inability in fallen man; thus, in salvation God received all the glory.

The reigning message of the Puritan preacher was:

> Conviction of sin, induced by the preaching of the Law, must precede faith, since no man will or can come to Christ to be saved from sin until he knows what sins he needs saving from.[42]

Packer, reviewing Puritan thought, continues:

---

[40] Thomas Watson, *Body of Divinity*, ed. George Rogers (1890; rpt. Grand Rapids: Baker Book House, 1979), p. 154.
[41] J. I. Packer, "Puritan Evangelism," *The Banner of Truth*, 9:8.
[42] *Ibid*, p. 10.

> It is the worst advice possible to tell a man to stop wor-
> rying about his sins and trust Christ at once if he does
> not know his sins and does not desire to leave them.[43]

From the doctrines of grace, the Puritans developed their
characteristic conception of the practice of evangelism. In
reviewing their evangelistic endeavors, Packer writes:

> Since God enlightens, convicts, humbles and converts
> through the Word, the task of His messengers is to
> communicate that Word, teaching and applying law and
> gospel. Preachers are to declare God's mind as set forth
> in the texts they expound to show the way of salvation,
> to exhort the unconverted to learn the law, to meditate
> on the Word, to humble themselves, to pray that God
> will show them their sins, and enable them to come to
> Christ.[44]

To the Puritan, evangelistic preaching was not a special
kind of preaching. It was a part of the ordinary, public ministry of God's Word. The Puritan pastor had the same quiet
confidence in the success of all his preaching. Knowing that
God's Word does not return void, they did not appear to engage in any feverish panic about it. They were firmly convinced that by the faithful preaching of the message of salvation God would call out the elect everywhere—not because
of the gifts or methods of the preacher, but by reason of
God's sovereign operation.

No point of Puritan theology is more delicate than that of
how much of man's effort is required in preparation for
grace. On this question hangs the whole biblical doctrine of
election. As an example of the plain and practical style of the

---

[43] *Ibid.*
[44] *Ibid,* p. 11.

Puritan preaching of sovereign grace, Thomas Hooker's handling of this problem was masterful in its simple approach through the terminology of play:

> The ball must first fall to the ground, before it can rebound back againe; for the Lord Jesus must first dart in his love into the soule, before the soule can rebound in love and joy to him againe, we must receive in grace before we can rebound backe any love to God: as I Tim. 1:7 . . . .[45]

While the doctrines of grace formed the backbone of their messages, discussion of that feature alone would minimize the glorious content of the whole counsel of God as presented by the Puritans. Granted, sovereign grace permeated every aspect of Puritan sermons, either in pressing upon the sinful the duties toward conversion or upon the saint the duties of mortifying the flesh. But let the Puritan divines speak for themselves and present their own case. Of all the many extracts one could select to illustrate the content of Puritan preaching, the following from Richard Sibbes must be considered one of the most comprehensive:

> To preach is to open the mystery of Christ, to open whatsoever is in Christ; to break open the box that the Saviour may be perceived of all. To open Christ's natures and Person what it is; to open the offices of Christ; first, he was a prophet to teach, wherefore he came into the world; then he was a priest, offering the sacrifice of himself; and then after he had offered his sacrifice as a priest, then was king. He was more publicly and gloriously known to be a king, to rule. After he had gained a people by his priesthood and offering, then

---

[45] Levy, p. 139.

he was to be a king to govern them . . . . He was all at the same time, but I speak in regard of manifestation. Now "to preach Christ" is to lay open all these things.

And likewise the states wherein he executed his office. First, the state of humiliation. Christ was first abased, and then glorified. The flesh he took upon him was first sanctified and then abased, and then he made it his glorious flesh. He could not work out our salvation but in a state of abasement; he could not apply it to us but in a state of exaltation and glory. To open the merits of Christ, what he hath wrought to his Father for us; to open his efficacy, as the spiritual head of his Church; what wonders he works in his children, by altering and raising of them, by fitting and preparing them for heaven; likewise to open all the promises in Christ, they are but Christ dished and parcelled out. "All the promises in Christ are yea and amen," 2 Cor. 1:20. They are made for Christ's sake, and performed for Christ's sake; they are all but Christ severed into so many particular gracious blessings. "To preach Christ" is to lay open all this, which is the inheritance of God's people.[46]

After speaking about the mysteries and offices of Christ, Sibbes discussed the need for proper application:

But it is not sufficient to preach Christ to lay open all this in the view of others; but in the opening of them, there must be application of them to the use of God's people, that they may see their interest in them; and there must be an alluring of them, for to preach is to woo. The preachers are "paraymphi," the friends of the bridegroom, that are to procure the marriage between Christ and his Church; therefore, they are not only to

---

[46] Richard Sibbes, *The Works of Richard Sibbes*, ed. Alexander B. Grosart, (2nd. ed.; 1862–64; rpt. Carlisle, Pa.: Banner of Truth, 1978), V:505–6.

open the riches of the husband, Christ, but likewise to
entreat for a marriage, and to use all the gifts and parts
that God hath given them, to bring Christ and his
Church together.[47]

Sibbes then addressed the issue of exposing one's inade-
quacy, and revealing the need for Christ as a vital ingredient
in sermon content:

And because people are in a contrary state to Christ, "to
preach Christ" is even to begin with the Law, to discover to people their estate by nature. A man can never
preach the gospel that makes no way for the gospel, by
showing and convincing people that they are out of
Christ. Who will marry with Christ, but those that
know their beggary and misery out of Christ? That he
must be had out of necessity, or else they die in debts
eternally; he must be had, or else they are eternally
miserable. Now when people are convinced of this,
then they make out of themselves to Christ. This,
therefore, must be done, because it is in order, that
which makes way to the preaching of Christ; for "the
full stomach despiseth an honeycomb," Prov. 27:7.
Who cares for balm that is not sick? Therefore, we see
John the Baptist came before Christ, to make way for
Christ, to level the mountains, to cast down whatsoever
exalts itself in man. He that is to preach must discern
what mountains there be between men's hearts and
Christ; and he must labour to discover themselves to
themselves, and lay flat all the pride of men in the dust;
for "the word of God is forcible to pull down
strongholds and imaginations and to bring all into subjection to Christ," 2 Cor. 10:4. And, indeed, though a
man should not preach the Law, yet by way of implication, all these things are wrapped in the gospel. What

---

[47] *Ibid.*

need of a Saviour, unless we are lost. What need of
Christ to be wisdom for us, if we were not fools in ourselves? What need Christ be sanctification to us, if we
were not defiled in ourselves? What need he be redemption, if we were not lost and sold in ourselves to
Satan, and under his bondage? Therefore all is to make
way for Christ, not only to open the mysteries of
Christ, but in opening and application to let us see the
necessity of Christ. In a word, being to bring Christ and
the Church together, our aim must be, to persuade
people to come out of their estate they are in, to come
and take Christ. Whatever makes for this, that course
we must use, though it be with never so much abasing
of ourselves.[48]

---

[48] *Ibid.*

Chapter 4

The Demands of Preaching

Nothing is clearer when reading Puritan literature than the realization that the Puritan preachers lived by a strong and abiding conviction of a vocation, and that they reveled in the task to which God had set them apart. This sense of vocation demanded a deep concern for personal piety in order to be faithful to the high calling of God in Christ Jesus. Yes, preaching had its glorious moments, but to these serious and devout men of the Word it also had its responsibilities. The weight of the load on them was as great as on any mortal man because of their understanding of who God was and the office He had sovereignly given them. Speaking to a group of fellow pastors, John Flavel cried:

> Believe it brethren, it is easier to declaim like an orator against a thousand sins of others than it is to mortify one sin like Christians in ourselves; to preach twenty sermons to our people than one to our own hearts.[1]

Jonathan Edwards believed that candidates for the ministry should be examined with respect to their principles and character as well as their religious beliefs and morals. In his farewell address to his congregation in Northampton, Edwards expressed the following concern for their future re-

---

[1] John Flavel, *The Works of John Flavel* (2nd. ed.; 1820; Carlisle, Pa.: Banner of Truth, 1968), VI:568.

garding the type of pastor they might call as his successor:

> Take care . . . that he be a man of thoroughly sound
> principles, in the scheme of doctrine which he main-
> tains. Labour to obtain a man who has an established
> character, as a person of serious religion and piety. If
> you should happen to settle a minister, who knows
> nothing, truly of Christ, and the way of salvation by
> Him, nothing experimentally of the nature of vital re-
> ligion; alas, how will you be exposed as sheep without a
> shepherd. You will need one that shall stand as a cham-
> pion in the cause of truth and godliness.[2]

Their view of God and His Church, of God and His
Word, of God and His messengers, gave the Puritan minister
the awesome judgment that an "erroneous or unfaithful minister was likely to do more hurt than good to the church."[3]

The demands for personal piety, a preaching to one's own
heart, can be best seen in the extended sermon on the demands of the ministry by Richard Baxter in his celebrated
work, *The Reformed Pastor*. This volume serves all ministers
as the classic model for ministerial consistency and faithfulness. Baxter originally prepared this work for a group of
Worcestershire preachers in December 1655.[4] In the first
chapter Baxter observes four main areas of the minister's life
that need constant surveillance. Concerning oneself, he
wrote:

[2] Jonathan Edwards, *The Works of Jonathan Edwards*, Rev. ed. Edward
Hickman (1834; rpt. Carlisle, Pa.: Banner of Truth, 1979), I:80.

[3] Ralph G. Turnbull, *Jonathan Edwards the Preacher* (Grand Rapids:
Baker Book House, 1958), p. 112.

[4] Richard Baxter, *The Reformed Pastor*, ed. William Brown (5th ed., 1656;
rpt. Carlisle, Pa.: Banner of Truth, 1979), p. 13.

Take heed to yourselves, lest you should be void of that saving grace of God, which you offer to others, and be stranger to the effectual workings of that gospel which you preach. . . . Many a preacher is now in hell, that hath a hundred times called upon his hearers to use the utmost care and diligence to escape it. . . . Believe it, brethren, God never saved any man for being a preacher, not because he was an able preacher; but because he was a justified, sanctified man, and consequently faithful in his master's work. Take heed therefore, to yourselves first, that you be that which you persuade your hearers to be.

Concerning the minister's personal conduct, Baxter exhorted:

Take heed to yourselves, lest you live in those actual sins which you preach against in others; and lest you be guilty of that which you condemn. . . . If sin be evil, why do you live in it? If it be not, why do you dissuade men from it?

Regarding their ministerial responsibilities:

Take heed to yourselves, that you be not unfit for the great employments that you have undertaken. He must not be himself a babe in knowledge that will teach all those mysterious things that are to be known in order to salvation. Oh, what qualifications are necessary for that man that hath such a charge upon him as we have! How many difficulties in divinity to be opened; yet about the fundamentals that must needs be known! How many obscure texts of Scripture to be expounded. . . . It is not now and then an idle snatch or taste of studies that will serve to make a sound divine. I know that laziness hath lately learned to pretend the lowness of all our studies, and how wholly and only the Spirit must qualify and assist to the work. . . . Oh, that men should dare so sinfully by their laziness to quench the Spirit; and then pretend the Spirit for the doing of it!

And then, tying together doctrine and example, Baxter admonished the pastor:

> Moreover, take heed to yourselves, lest your example contradict your doctrine, and lest you lay such stumbling-blocks before the blind, as may be the occasion of their ruin; lest you may unsay that with your lives, which you say with your tongues; and be the greatest hinderers of the success of your own labours. . . . One proud, surly, lordly word, one needless contention, one covetous action, may cut the throat of many a sermon, and blast the fruit of all that you have been doing. . . . We must study as hard now to live well, as how to preach well.[5]

"We must study as hard how to live well as how to preach well" summarized the demands that the Puritan pastor placed paramount in his fulfilling the high calling of an expositor of God's Word. When they referred to the demands of the ministry, they did not think of the amount of time given in actual ministry situations, but rather of the requirements of time and effort in "the oversight of ourselves."[6] Ministry, to the Puritans, was an overflow of what God had given to them in the beauties of their relationship with the living Lord. Thus, times of actual ministry were never considered a burden, but a joy in sharing in God's ministry to the lost in the great work of gathering His Church.

Equal demand was placed upon their sermon preparation

---

[5] *Ibid*, pp. 53–71.
[6] *Ibid*, p. 53.

as upon their personal piety. Baxter gave us an indication of what preaching should be when he penned these words:

> What skill is necessary to make plain the truth, to convince the hearers; to let in the unresistable light in to their consciences, and to keep it there, and drive all home; to screw the truth into their minds, and work Christ into their affections; to meet every objection that gainsays, and clearly to resolve it; to drive sinners to a stand and make them see there is no hope, but they may unavoidably be converted or condemned; and to do all this so for language and manner as beseems our work, and yet as is most suitable to the capacities of our hearers: this, and a great deal more should be done in every sermon, should surely be done with a great and holy skill. So great a God, whose message we declare, should be honoured by our delivery of it.[7]

In reality, though, their preparation was an extension of the personal relationship to God through the Scriptures. The demands of the preaching office on the lives of these men included strenuous day-to-day labor. Preaching several times a week, generally twice on the Lord's day, one lecture during mid-week, and other occasions which were seasonal, time was of the essence. A remarkable insight is given from the life of George Whitefield into the difficulty of finding study time adequate for their high standards. Dallimore recalls from the life of the great evangelist this picture:

> There he is at five in the morning, in the room above the Harris book-store. He is on his knees with the English Bible, his Greek New Testament and *Henry's Commentary* spread out before him. He reads a portion in English, gains a fuller insight into it as he studies

---

[7] *Ibid*, p. 70.

words and tenses in the Greek, and then considers
Matthew Henry's explanation of it all. Finally, there
comes the unique practice that he has developed; that of
"praying over every line word" of both the English and
the Greek till the passage, in its essential message, has
veritably become part of his own soul.[8]

Dallimore continues this amazing illustration of the duality of piety and sermon preparation, the latter being the
overflow of the former:

Such was Whitefield's study of the Bible in the months
following his conversion. There were branches of
learning to which he gave little or no attention, but he
concentrated on the all-important Word of God. When,
in later chapters, we see him preaching forty and more
hours a week, with little or no time for preparation, we
may well look back on these days in Gloucester and recognize that he was then laying up a store of Biblical
knowledge on which he was able to draw amidst the
haste and tumult of such a ministry.[9]

The iron discipline that characterized the Puritan style of
life no doubt played a significant part in the success of their
ministries. Lewis cites William Attersol in describing the
discipline required as well as the cost exacted:

For this, if we know not by practice, we may see by experience that to study with constantness, to instruct
with diligence, to exhort with carefulness, to reprove
with zeal, to comfort with cheerfulness, to convince
with boldness, to watch over the people with a godly

---

8 Arnold A. Dallimore, *George Whitfield* (Westchester, Il.: Cornerstone
Books, 1979), I:83.
9 *Ibid.*

oversight, as they must give account for their souls, to
conceive godly anger and great sorrow for sin, to pray in
public and private, to go in and out before the people of
God in the doctrine of faith, and in the example of life,
to prepare themselves to handle the Word, and to deliver it with proper power and evidence of the Spirit,
and with earnest affections; being thus prepared, I say,
to perform all these duties doth more consume the inward parts, waste the body, impair nature, decay
strength, spend the vital spirits, and cause them to be
subject to sundry infirmities, sickness and diseases than
any of the strongest labour that is used among men.[10]

As far as the Puritans were concerned, Attersol's picture
of the faithful pastor was not unrealistic or overly idealistic.
To them, it was as truly possible as it was truly admired.[11]
John Flavel has left us with an intimate glimpse of the
heart of the Puritan pastor as it relates to his personal oversight and the subsequent accomplishments in the ministry:

How many truths we have to study! How many wiles of
Satan and mysteries of corruption to detect! How many
cases of conscience to resolve! Yea, we must fight in de-
fence of the truths we preach, as well as study them to
paleness, and preach them unto faithfulness: but well-
spent: head, heart, lungs and all; welcome pained
breasts, aching backs, and trembling legs; if we can all
but approve ourselves Christ's faithful servants, and
hear that joyful voice from his mouth, "Well done, good
and faithful servants!"[12]

---

[10] Peter Lewis, *The Genius of Puritanism* (Morgan, Pa.: Soli Deo Gloria,
1995), p. 46.

[11] *Ibid.*

[12] Flavel, VI:569.

Charles Spurgeon, often referred to as "the last of the Puritans" by historians, charged the members of the Pastor's College, which he founded for the purpose of equipping great preachers, with the following exhortation:

> If we are to pursue our holy calling with success, we need to be better men. Brethren, I do not depreciate you; far from it. But, personally, I feel that, as the times grow sterner, I must cry to God for more grace, that I may be more able to cope with them. Brethren, let it be a main business with us to be ourselves more holy, more gracious, and therefore better fitted for our work. Let us not judge ourselves by others, and say, with deadening self-complacency, "We are getting on well as compared with our brethren." Let us measure ourselves by our Master, and not by our fellow-servants: then pride will be impossible, but hopefulness will be natural.[13]

On another occasion before the same body, Spurgeon concluded an address with this comment: "Your object is, however, so to bear your personal witness that others may be convinced thereby of the truth of what is so sure to your own soul."[14] Indeed, that is a concise statement regarding the Puritan minister's understanding of the real relationship between his personal holiness and the success of his ministry. Because of their view of God, and their subsequent understanding of their position as a pastor on display before their holy Mentor, these men took very seriously their own oversight.

In a sermon entitled "How the Uncharitable and

---

[13] Charles Spurgeon, *An All Round Ministry* (4th ed.; 1900; rpt. Carlisle, Pa.: Banner of Truth, 1978), p.302–3.
[14] *Ibid*, p. 321.

Dangerous Contentions That Are Among Professors of the True Religion May Be Allayed," Richard Steele applied his sermon to himself as well as his audience when he stated:

> Apply yourselves to the practice of real piety. By this I mean, that we should employ our chief care to procure and increase a lively faith, to exercise daily repentance, to strengthen our hope, to inflame our love to God and to our neighbor, to grow in humility, zeal, patience, and self-denial: to be more diligent in watchfulness over our thoughts, words, ways, in mortification of our sinful passions and affections, in the examination of our spiritual estate, in meditation, in secret and fervent prayer, and in universal and steady obedience. In these things do run the vital spirits of religion: and whoso is seriously employed in these, will have but little time, and less mind, for unnecessary contentions. These will keep that heat about the heart, which, evaporating, degenerates into airy and fiery exhalations, and leaves the soul as cold as ice to any holy desires.[15]

The Puritans thought that if they were busily and faithfully given to the business of personal piety by observing their own estate before God, they would have less occupation with the things of this world that might detract from their high calling as a proclaimer of the biblical message. Few, if any, express the magnitude of this mindset with more clarity and intensity than Richard Baxter. The whole first chapter of his *Reformed Pastor* is given to this priority. He devoted some of the most potent of his forceful writings to eight reasons why a pastor should constantly examine his state and confirm his standing before God:

---

15 *Puritan Sermons: 1659-1689* (Wheaton: Richard Owen Roberts, 1981), IV:248.

You have a heaven to win or lose yourselves. Believe it sirs, God is no respecter of persons: he saveth not men for their coats or callings; a holy calling will not save an unholy man.

Take heed to yourselves, for you have a depraved nature, and sinful inclinations, as well as others. Alas! even in our hearts as well as in our hearers, there is an averseness to God. Those treacherous hearts will at one time or another deceive you, if you take heed not. Those sins that seem to lie dead, will revive: your pride and worldliness, and many a noisome vice will spring up, that you thought had been weeded out by the roots.

And the rather, take heed to yourselves, because such works as ours do put men on greater use and trial of their graces, and have greater temptations, than many other men's. It is not only the work that calls for heed but the workman also, that he may be fit for business of such weight.

And the rather, also, take heed to yourselves, because the tempter will make his first or sharpest onset upon you. He beareth you the greatest malice, that are engaged to do him the greatest mischief . . . he knows what a rout he may make among the rest, if the leaders fall before their eyes. You shall have his most subtle insinuations, and incessant solicitations, and violent assaults. As wise and learned as you are, take heed to yourselves lest he outwit you. The devil is a greater scholar than you, and a nimbler disputant . . . he will play the juggler with you undiscerned, and cheat you of your faith or innocency, and you shall not know that you have lost it; nay, he will make you believe it is multiplied or increased when it is lost.

Take heed to yourselves also, because there are many eyes upon you, and therefore there will be many observers of your fall. You cannot miscarry but the world

will ring of it. The eclipses of the sun by daytime are
seldom without witness. Take heed therefore to yourselves, and do your works as those that remember that
the world looks on them, and that with the quick-
sighted eye of malice, ready to make the worst of all, and
to find the smallest fault where it is, and aggravate it
where they find it, and divulge it, and make advantageous
to their designs; and to make faults where they cannot
find them. How cautiously then should we walk before
so many ill-minded observers!

Take heed to yourselves; for your sins have more
heinous aggravations than other men's. It is noted
among King Alphonsus' saying, That a great man cannot
commit a small sin. You are likelier than others to sin
against knowledge, because you have more than they.
Your sins have more hypocrisy in them than other
men's by how much the more you have spoken against
them.

Take heed to yourselves; for the honour of your Lord
and Master, and of his holy truth and ways, doth more
lie on you than on other men. As you may do him more
service, so also more disservice than others. The nearer
men stand to God, the greater dishonour hath he by
their miscarriages; and the more will they be imputed
by foolish men to God himself.

Take heed to yourselves; for the souls of your hearers,
and the success of your labors, do very much depend
upon it. God useth to fit great men for great works before he will make them his instruments in accomplishing them.[16]

To the Puritans, one who did not "preach to his own
heart" could not preach effectively to others. The demands

---

[16] Baxter, pp. 72–86.

of the ministry of preaching began with themselves in the demands for their own piety. To them, it was a very logical reasoning that this should be so. Again, as stated by Baxter, "If the work of the Lord be not soundly done upon your own hearts, how can you expect that he bless your labours for the effecting of it in others?"[18]

---

[18] *Ibid*, p. 80.

Chapter 5

The Duties of the Pastor

The view of the pulpit held by the Puritans not only determined the direction of their preaching and dictated the demands on the preacher, but it also defined their pastoral duties. To the Puritans, pastoral work was not taken lightly, but was viewed as an integral part of the work of the preacher. These men, who placed such a high priority on the sermon as the center of their worship, saw their pastoral duties as the personal application of the sermon to the individuals within their flocks. Pastoral ministry was, to these great under-shepherds of God's flock, the means by which the truths of the sermon were applied to the hearers whom the sermon reached. Richard Baxter captures in great detail the Puritan spirit in this ministry of overseeing the flock:

> Take heed to all the flock; it is, you see, all the flock, or every individual member of our charge. To this end it is necessary, that we should know every person that belongeth to our charge; for how can we take heed of them, if we do not know them? We must labour to be acquainted, not only with the persons, but with the state of all our people, with their inclinations and conversations; what are the sins of which they are most in danger, and what duties they are most apt to neglect, and what temptations they are liable to; for if we know not their temperament or disease, we are not likely to prove successful physicians.[1]

---

[1] Richard Baxter, *The Reformed Pastor*, ed. William Brown (5th ed., 1656;

The Puritan preachers saw the ministry of oversight not as something desirable, but as a matter of sacred and downright serious business.[2] John Flavel correlated the ministry in the pulpit with the ministry of oversight:

> A prudent minister will study the souls of his people, more than the best human books in his library; and not chuse what is easiest for him, but what is most necessary for them. Ministers that are acquainted with the state of their flocks, as they ought to be, will be seldom at a loss in the choice of the next subject; their people's wants will chuse their text, from time to time, for them.[3]

In the same sermon ("The Character of a Complete Evangelical Pastor"), Flavel exhorted his fellow pastors:

> Take heed to your ministry that you fulfill it: take heed to yourselves, and to the flocks over which the Holy Ghost hath made you overseers. Let us study and preach, let us pray and converse among our people, that we may both save ourselves, and them that hear us.[4]

The Puritans considered themselves watchmen over the flock. Prayer for the individuals in the congregation was a vital ingredient in the fulfilling of such responsibilities. John Owen's statement, "He that is more frequent in his pulpit to his people than he is in his closet for his people is

---

rpt. Carlisle, Pa.: Banner of Truth, 1979), p. 90.

[2] Peter Lewis, *The Genius of Puritanism* (Morgan, Pa.: Soli Deo Gloria, 1995), p. 63.

[3] John Flavel, *The Works of John Flavel* (2nd. ed.; 1820; Carlisle, Pa.: Banner of Truth, 1968), VI:571.

[4] *Ibid*, p. 58.

but a sorry watchman,"[5] clearly reveals the heart of the Puritan preacher for the well-being of his sheep.

Charles Spurgeon, a man greatly affected by the life and ministry of the Puritans, although not ministering within the classical Puritan era, reflected this faithful attitude of the Puritan mindset in their shepherding duties:

> If we should be faithful as stewards, we must not neglect any one of the family, nor neglect any portion of the estate. I wonder whether we practise a personal observation of our hearers. London needs not only house to house visitation, but room to room visitation. We must in the case of our people go further, and practise man-to-man visitation. By personal intercourse alone, can certain persons be reached. We must watch over our sheep one by one. This is to be done not only by personal talk, but by personal prayer.
>
> We ought thus to beat the bounds of our parish, and go round and round our congregations, forgetting none, despairing of none, bearing all upon our hearts before the Lord. Especially let us think of the poor, the crotchety, the desponding. Let our care, like the hurdles of a sheepfold, enclose all the flock.[6]

It was with his pastoral character that the Puritan minister watched for souls, "as one that must give account" (Hebrews 13:17 KJV).

Although not a Puritan himself, Charles Bridges cited the pastoral mindset of several Puritans in the chapter "The Pastoral Work" in his classic *The Christian Ministry*:

---

[5] I.D.E. Thomas, comp. ed., *A Puritan Golden Treasury* (Carlisle, Pa.: Banner of Truth, 1977), p. 191.

[6] Charles Spurgeon, *An All Round Ministry* (4th ed., 1900; rpt. Carlisle, Pa.: Banner of Truth, 1978), p. 275.

Calvin often lays down the Scriptural obligation to this work, and reports the fruitful harvests reaped at Geneva, when the ministers and elders went from house to house, and dealt closely and individually with the consciences of the people. Kidderminster, before Baxter's coming there, was like a piece of dry and barren earth; but by the blessing of heaven upon his labours, the face of Paradise, appeared there in all the fruits of righteousness. Alleine often did bless God for the great success he had in these exercises, saying that God had made him as instrumental of good to souls this way as by public preaching, if not more. Cotton Mather, while he looked upon this work as laborious as any in all the Ministry, yet set a great value upon his Pastoral visits. He not only did, but got good in his conversations with all sorts of persons, and thought he never walked more in the Spirit, than thus walking to his flock, to serve and seek their best interests.[7]

Peter Lewis has captured the misunderstanding of this aspect of the Puritan preacher when he states, "Provocative as it may appear, it must be said that among the Puritans . . . pastoral work was not the light and uncertain thing which it has largely become in our own day."[8]

Because the Puritans took their pulpit responsibilities so seriously, they regarded their pastoral duties with equal earnestness; the latter was the means of making personal application of the former. The means of accomplishing such duties were catechizing, counseling, comforting, and communing in private times of worship with individuals within the flock.

---

[7] Charles Bridges, *The Christian Ministry* (4th ed.; 1830; rpt. Carlisle, Pa.: Banner of Truth, 1980), p. 348.
[8] Lewis, p. 63.

Catechizing the People

"The very insistence that sermons 'should not die at their birth,' " says Horton Davies, "was characteristic of the Puritan zeal for edification."[9] No greater expression of this aspect of preaching can be seen than in the Puritan emphasis on the examination of families by the popular question-and-answer method on points of doctrinal and practical divinity,[10] known as "catechizing."

Again, Baxter must be cited as the clearest example of this Puritan theory of ministerial oversight of the sheep. He gave a revealing example of the need for such activity:

> I am daily forced to admire how lamentably ignorant many of our own people are, that have seemed diligent hearers of men these ten or twelve years, while I spoke as plainly as I was able to speak. Some know not that each person in the Trinty is God; nor that Christ is God and man; nor that he took his human nature with him into heaven; nor many like the necesary principles of our faith. Yea, some that come constantly to public meetings are grossly ignorant; whereas in one hour's familiar instruction of them in private, they seem to understand more, and better entertain it, than they did in all their lives before. We spend Monday and Tuesday from morning to almost night in the work; besides a chapelry, catechized by another assistant; taking about fifteen or sixteen families in a week, that we may go through the parish, which hath about eight-hundred families, in a year.[11]

This concept lay deep in the Puritan influence wherever

---

9 Horton Davies, *The Worship of the English Puritans* (Morgan, Pa.: Soli Deo Gloria, 1997), p. 196.
10 Lewis, p. 63.
11 Baxter, p. 43.

it was found, and was a point of emphasis in many of their sermons. As part of the monthly morning exercises at Giles in the Fields near London, Thomas Woodcock challenged his fellow ministers in a sermon entitled, "On Heaven." He said that the true minister's trusteeship in keeping the truths of God was by catechizing and instilling these principles into the hearts of young ones. Foundation-stones must be laid with great exactness and care; for they support the whole building. In that sermon, Woodcock stated that the other means of keeping these truths was assiduous preaching.[12]

Even more explicit detail is uncovered in a sermon by Thomas Lyle as part of a similar series of morning lectures held at Cripplegate. Lyle expounded in a rather lengthy sermon entitled, "By What Scriptural Rules May Catechizing Be So Managed as That It May Become Universally Profitable?" He preached on the precept, the promise, the important duty of and the persuasive motives of this form of instruction. His chosen text was Proverbs 22:6, "Train up a child in the way he should go, and when he is old, he will not depart from it." True to the sermon construction characteristic of the Puritans, Lyle first stated the doctrine to be reasoned and then applied it. The doctrine stated by Lyle is that "it is the great and indispensable duty, and therefore ought to be the serious and constant care, of superiors, prudently and piously to train up or catechise, to instruct and educate, all such inferiors as are committed to their care and conduct." He then outlined the sermon content in the following divisions:

---

[12] *Puritan Sermons: 1659-1689* (Wheaton: Richard Owen Roberts, 1981), V:522.

I. What it is to train up or catechise.
II. What is meant by that "way" wherein persons are to be trained up.
III. Who they are, that are to be trained up or catechized.
IV. Who they are that are to train up or catechize, and why.
V. How the whole affair may be so prudently, piously, spiritually managed, as that it may be crowned with such a blessed success, as to become most universally profitable.[13]

Great detail is given to each point, revealing the heart of these men for the application of the Scriptures to become more than just something people heard in a sermon, but to become the means by which they lived their entire lives. Perhaps no greater illustration exists of the Puritan view of the authority of the Word of God than in the efforts of catechism as a support to their pulpit ministry.

One finds it interesting to note that Lyle did not limit the word "child" to mean a youngster, but rather stated, "Who they are that are thus to be trained up or catechised? All younger ones and inferiors that are committed by God or men to the care and conduct of superiors; all included in the name child."[14] Spurgeon picked up on this idea of catechizing all the flock, not just children, when he said:

> I will give you a little advice, which may be suitable for such a time as this. I would recommend you to go over the fundamental truths with all your hearers very carefully. The bulk of the people do not know the first principle of the gospel. We assume too much when we

---

13 *Puritan Sermons: 1659-1689*, II:100.
14 *Ibid*, p. 101.

take it for granted that our hearers, all of them, understand the gospel.[15]

The value of such a supportive ministry to the preaching
of the Puritans may be seen in the exhaustive ministry of
Richard Baxter of Kidderminster. Packer evaluates the faith
of such labors in Baxter:

> This was the faith that God honoured in Richard
> Baxter's Kidderminster ministry, during which, over a
> period of seventeen years, by the use of no other means
> but sermons twice a week and catechetical instruction
> from house to house, well over six hundred converts
> were gathered in; of whom Baxter wrote, six years after
> his ejection, that, despite constant exposure to ridicule
> and obloquy for their "Puritanism," "not one that I
> know of has fallen off from his sincerity."[16]

Counseling the Perplexed

Lewis states that "the counselling work of the Puritan
pastor largely involved settling the consciences of troubled
Christians and of persons as yet unconverted but who were
convicted of sin and seeking to know more of the way of salvation."[17] In the volumes of Puritan literature on spiritual
depression, most often the causes of these periods of a sense
of the loss of the presence of God were attributed to an im-
balance of love, grace, and power within the believer. The
common term to describe such a state was a "desertion." By
this or other common phrases ("the dark night of the soul" or
"the soul's wintertime") they did not mean that God had totally deserted the elect soul, but that a real sense of His pres-

---

[15] Spurgeon, p. 308.
[16] J. I. Packer, "Puritan Evangelism," *The Banner of Truth*, 9:12–13.
[17] Lewis, p. 63.

ence was denied the believer for a reason known only to
God.[18] The present work is not designed to dwell on the
subject of the condition of spiritual desertions and depressions, but it is a fascinating area of the Puritan mindset.
There are sufficient works covering this informative subject,
especially Richard Baxter's other massive work, *A Christian
Directory* (published by Soli Deo Gloria). The book is a comprehensive insight into the Puritan pastor's ability to handle
such concerns.

Much of the counseling ministry of the Puritans came as a
result of the catechizing of the families of their congregations. Because so much emphasis was laid upon the heart of
the Puritan pastor to be able to read his people as he would
read a book, spiritual depressions or queries unto salvation
were easily discerned. On the one hand, the style of
preaching offered by the Puritans created or fostered such
concerns or inquiries; but because of their deep conviction
that the Word preached must be applied they became
equally adept at relieving such pain of soul in the true believer as well as applying the balm of salvation to the lost. In
the annals of history, the healing ministry of the Puritan
pastors has been lost, giving way to the modern evaluation of
their ministry as being imbalanced in favor of Sinai and not
enough Calvary. Reading countless Puritan sermons has
caused this writer to conclude that they preached with equal
fervor the peace of the gospel as well as the terrors of the
law. To the Puritans, such travails caused by their preaching
were a necessary part of the new birth or a preparation for
evidence of God's greater visitation and mercy in the
future.[19] Concerning spiritual desertions, Flavel counseled:

---

[18] *Ibid*, p. 66.
[19] *Ibid*, p. 64.

Oh, prepare for spiritual troubles; I am sure you do enough every day to involve you in darkness. Now, if at any time this trial befall you, mind these two seasonable admonitions, and lay them up for such a time. First, exercise the faith of adherence, when you have lost the faith of evidence. When God takes away that, he leaves this: that is necessary to the comfort, this to the life of his people. It is sweet to live in views of your interest, but if they be gone, believe and rely on God, for an interest. Stay yourselves on your God when you have no light, Isa. 1:10. Drop this anchor in the dark, and do not reckon all gone when evidence is gone: never reckon yourselves undone whilst you can adhere to your God. Direct acts are noble acts of faith, as well as reflexive ones; yea, and in some respects to be preferred to them. Faith of evidence brings more joy to you, but faith of adherence brings more glory to God: for thereby you must trust him when you cannot see him; yea, you believe not only without, but against sense and feeling; and, doubtless, that which brings glory to God, is better than that which brings comfort to you.

Take the right method to recover the sweet light which you have sinned away from your souls. Do not go about from one to another complaining; nor yet sit down desponding under your burden. But, first, search diligently after the cause of God's withdrawment; urge him hard, by prayer, to tell thee wherefore he contends with thee.[20]

Robert Bolton addressed the issue of the perils of the unconverted actually fostered by their preaching:

It is the only right everlasting method to turn men from darkness to light, from the power of Satan unto God: and all the men of God and master-builders who

---

[20] Flavel, I:417–18.

have ever set themselves sincerely to serve God in their
ministry and to save souls, have followed the same
course, to wit: First, to wound by the Law, and then to
heal by the Gospel. We must be humbled in the sight
of the Lord before he lift us up, Jam. 4:10. We must be
sensible of our spiritual blindness, captivity, poverty before we can heartily seek to be savingly enlightened.
There must be sense of misery before showing of
mercy; crying "I am unclean, I am unclean" before
opening up the fountain for uncleanness . . . brokenness
of heart before building up.[21]

Continuing further in his sermon, Bolton demonstrates the
heart of Puritan counseling—the application of the mercy
after the fostering of the misery—when he tenderly said:

The mercy of God is like himself, infinite: all our sins
are finite, both in number and nature. Now, between
finite and infinite there is no proportion, and so no
possibility of resistance. And therefore be thy sins
never so notorious and numberless, yet (in a truly broken heart, thirsting for and throwing itself upon Christ,
unfeignedly resolving upon new obedience and his glorious service for the time to come) thy sins can no more
withstand or stand before God's mercies than a little
spark the boundless and mighty ocean, thrown into it,
infinitely less. Our desires of grace, faith and repentance, are the graces themselves which we desire, at
least in God's acceptation, who accepteth the will for
the deed, and our affections for the actions.[24]

Counseling was an extension of catechizing, as catechizing
was an extension of preaching the whole council of God.
Thus, the plain style of the Puritan sermon was taken to fur-

---

[21] Lewis, p. 64–65.
[24] *Ibid*, p. 65.

ther depths of understanding and application in the pastoral side of their ministry.

Comforting the Person
The degree of their pastoral ministry continued to go deeper as the Puritan pastor was about the business of visitation in fulfilling his sacred calling. It was in this comforting work that we see that they were truly physicians of the soul. Lewis remarks:

> The Puritans were physicians of the soul, skilled enough to avoid that vagueness and subjectiveness which leaves the anguished mind clutching at uncertain straws with uncertain hope. They believed the Word of God to be comprehensive enough to cover every basic human situation and need, and knew their Scriptures well enough to apply, with responsible authority, the available salve to the exposed sore.[23]

Just as they approached the pulpit in an unalterably biblical and solidly dogmatic way, the Puritan ministers dealt with a confused believer in a similar fashion. Because of their view of the pulpit, they understood that the ministry did not end with the spoken word. Jean Daille underscores this thought with the statement, "Ministers are not cooks, but physicians, and therefore should not study to delight the palate, but to recover the patient."[24] In this ministry the Puritans excelled, as they applied their sermon messages to the hearts of their people. Lewis makes this observation concerning these Puritan preacher-physicians:

---

[23] *Ibid.*
[24] Thomas, p. 190.

They were also clear, logical and fearless enough to set
before the confused believer his or her state in an orderly fashion, quietly and clearly making the "patient"
understand his particular distress, what it issued from,
and where relief from it lay. People were thus turned
back from side-issues and from obsession with mere
symptoms to the real needs and proper resorts of the
soul in that condition.[25]

A sermon entitled "How Ministers or Christian Friends
May and Ought to Apply Themselves to Sick Friends, for
Their Good, and the Discharge of Their Own Conscience,"
by Matthew Poole, reveals the seriousness with which the
Puritans considered this aspect of their calling:

Many act as if they thought this were all the work of a
minister, to make a few sermons, read some prayers,
etc. No, no; a minister must be "thoroughly furnished
to every good work." He must be apt and able for every
good work; this, among others. O what angelical abilities
doth it require! Acuteness, to discern the sick man's
temper; knowledge, to understand the nature of all spiritual diseases, the symptoms, the prognostics, as also the
antidotes and remedies; wisdom to make suitable, speedy
aplications. O how hard a case it is! Many a sick man can
neither endure . . . neither the disease of their souls,
nor their "remedy," etc. A minister had need know all
things, understand all persons, discern the subtilities of
men's hearts, and not be ignorant of the wiles of the
devil.

O the difficulty! It is a sad thing to consider, that many
souls do perish, not only "by the force of their disease,"
but also "by the error of their physician," by the mis-
takes of their ministers. A small error there, may occa-

---

[25] Lewis, p. 65.

sion fearful mischief; so a small mistake in soul's con-
cernments may occasion a soul's everlasting ruin.[26]

John Flavel echoed this call to a comforting ministry in a
sermon where he listed "the duties enjoined on them
[ministers] in the Scripture, in the conscientious Discharge
whereof, they receive signal Fruits of his Favour."[27]
According to Flavel, "Their ninth duty is, not only to relieve
the distressed members of Christ, but to seek out, and visit
them; to know their spiritual and temporal wants, in order to
a full discharge of that duty; Jam. 1:27."[28]
It was in the honesty of the Puritan approach to comforting their flock that we see the true skill of these men.
Because of their confidence in the power of God's creative
word, they were direct in their efforts to identify the cause
of such a soul condition; but they were equally direct in
offering Christ as the all-sufficient Comforter. In a sermon
on the work of the means and measure of bruising, and the
comfort to ones in such condition, Richard Sibbes compas-
sionately said:

> For the concluding of this point, and our encouragement
> to a thorough work of bruising, and patience under God's
> bruising us, let us all know that none are fitter for com-
> fort than those that think themselves furthest off.
> Men, for the the most part, are not lost enough in their
> own feeling for a Saviour. A holy despair in ourselves is
> the ground of true hope, Hos. 14:3. In God the father-
> less find mercy: if men were more fatherless, they
> should feel more God's fatherly affection from heaven;
> for God that dwelleth in the highest heaven, Isa. 36:2,

---

26 *Puritan Sermons: 1659-1689*, I:120.
27 Flavel, VI:588.
28 *Ibid.*

dwelleth likewise in the lowest soul. Christ's sheep are
weak sheep, and wanting in something or other: he
therefore applieth himself to the necessities of every
sheep.[29]

In another sermon entitled "The Soul's Conflict," the
tender Sibbes affirmed the ministry of the body of Christ in
comforting one another by saying: "God often suspends
comfort from us to drive us to make use of our Christian
friends, by whom he purposeth to do us good."[30] Later in
the same sermon, Sibbes admonished his fellow pastors that
for them not to be a part of the ministry of comforting the
distressed would be a sinful mark on their calling.[31]

John Howe preached a sermon on Colossians 2:2, "That
Their Hearts May Be Comforted," and succinctly summarized the purpose of the comforting ministry of Puritan
pastors:

> In short, the end which the apostle aims at, the comfort
> intended to these Christians, was their establishment
> and confirmed state in their Christianity, as the effect
> of all apostolical or ministerial exhortations, persuasions,
> encouragements, or any whatsoever endeavours; made
> efficacious to that purpose by the powerful influence
> and operation of the Holy Ghost.[32]

The intent of the pastoral ministry was not limited to
alleviating the symptoms of the discomfort or distress, but to
establishing a stronger relationship to Christ by faith.

---

[29] Richard Sibbes, *The Works of Richard Sibbes*, ed. Alexander B. Grosart,
(2nd. ed., 1862-64; rpt. Carlisle, Pa.: Banner of Truth, 1973), I:48.
[30] *Ibid*, p. 195.
[31] *Ibid.*
[32] *Puritan Sermons: 1659-1689*, III:84.

In another sermon delivered as part of the Cripplegate Morning Exercises, William Whitaker spoke for his fellow Puritans in revealing Christ as the source of all comfort: "Christ is all, to fill every condition with comfort. The best of conditions is not good without him, nor is the worst bad with him."[33]

The understanding the Puritan preachers had of the pulpit being the means that God might sovereignly use to expose and bruise the soul defined the kind of pastoral counseling ministry they would have—one that would lead the despondent to the cross and the comfort of the Savior.

Communing in Private Worship

Quite often, the Puritan pastor would celebrate special times of private worship with certain families or groups of friends as part of his pastoral ministry. These services generally took place on what were known as "fast-days" or "thanksgiving-days." Lewis illustrates this ministry in the life of Oliver Heywood, quoting from one of the pastor's diaries:

> Friday: we had a solemn day of fasting and prayer in my sister's house, God wonderfully assisted, there was a considerable number of people. Mr. Starkey prayed, I preached and prayed four hours. Oh, what a flame was my heart in.[34]

There were several uses for this type of ministry. Private meetings with particular families or groups were conducted to review the previous week's sermon in order to make proper application. Other times were used with the young

---

[33] *Ibid*, I:508–9.
[34] Lewis, p. 66.

people to instruct them in such disciplines as prayer and personal meditation over the Scripture.[35]

In many instances, the services held on the special or private fast-days were known to have consumed the entire day. John Howe's practice with the flock at Great Torrington, Devon was indicative of such lengthy times of worship.

> It was upon these occasions his common way to begin about nine in the morning with prayer for about a quarter hour in which he begged a blessing on the work of the day: and afterwards read and expounded a chapter or psalm in which he spent three-quarters of an hour. Then he prayed for about an hour, preached for another hour and prayed for about half an hour. After this he retired and took some little refreshment for about a quarter of an hour more (the people singing all the while) and then came again into the pulpit and prayed for another hour and gave them another sermon of about an hour's length, and so concluded the service of the day at about four of the clock in the evening with about half an hour or more in prayer.[36]

Other Puritan divines were known for services of similar length. Matthew Henry records that his father, Philip Henry, "begun at nine o'clock and never stirred out of the pulpit till about four o'clock in the evening, spending all the time in praying, expounding, singing, and preaching to the admiration of all that heard him."[37] Many local Puritan congregations would attend other churches' fast-day services when their own church did not have such a service.

Peter Lewis mentions an example taken from Benjamin

---

[35] Davies, pp. 200–201.
[36] Lewis, p. 60.
[37] *Ibid*, p. 61.

Brook's work, *The Lives of the Puritans* (reprinted by Soli Deo Gloria), concerning the ministry of Stephen Marshall:

> Mr. Marshall frequently united with his brethren in the observation of public fasts, when the services were usually protracted to a very great length. On one of these occasions, it is said, that Dr. Twisse having commenced the public service with a short prayer, Mr. Marshall prayed in a wonderful pathetic and prudent manner for two hours. Mr. Arrowsmith then preached an hour, then they sung a psalm after which Mr. Vines prayed nearly two hours; Mr. Palmer preached an hour and Mr. Seaman prayed nearly two hours; Mr. Henderson then spoke of the evils of the time and how they were to be remedied, and Dr. Twisse closed the service with a short prayer.[38]

Puritan pastors observed private as well as national fast-days. Oftentimes the more private fasts were conducted in the presence of a dozen or so people in a private home. The more lengthy services were conducted on the national days of fasting and were of a more public fashion. Matthew Barker described a religious fast as:

> The devotion of the whole man to a solemn, extraordinary attendance upon God, in a particular time separated for that end, for the depreciation of his displeasure, and for the supplicating of his favour, joined with an abstinence from bodily food, and other bodily delights, and from secular affairs.[39]

Continuing in his message, this Puritan preacher reached the heart of the reason for such frequent acts of worship:

---

[38] *Ibid.*
[39] *Puritan Sermons: 1659-1689*, II:149.

> So he that fasteth doth for that time separate himself to
> God, and doth voluntarily dedicate a part of time to his
> more solemn service; and doth put himself, as it were,
> under a religious vow, to abide solemnly with God in the
> duties of the fast he is engaged in.[40]

Separation unto God was a hallmark of the Puritan life-
style, and Puritan ministers used the fast as a means of
strengthening this concept in the minds of their flocks.
Consistent with this application was another mentioned in
the concluding remarks of the sermon by Barker:

> Fasting ought to be followed with sincere and universal
> reformation; else it avails nothing. If moral duties be
> neglected, the practice of the strictest institutions is
> unacceptable to God.[41]

Communing in private worship was another part of the
pastoral ministry of the Puritan preachers to aid their flocks
in becoming approved unto God as His separate people by
applying the truth of God's Word preached the previous
Lord's Day from the pulpit.

---

[40] *Ibid.*
[41] *Ibid*, p. 164.

Chapter 6

Conclusion

The spirit of this age would have us believe that the avenue of preaching is no longer the means by which God will revive His Church. Rather, we are to engage in and enlist more contemporary means to accomplish what God has said He would do through the foolishness of preaching. More ritual with attention to ceremony, or one or more of the many forms of entertainment—films, music, drama, and testimones—are the answers to the ineffectiveness of the church, we are told. Yet others will say that the need of the hour is small groups, where we can relate to one another and share our concerns. In such an era as this, a study of the Puritan view of the pulpit is like a refreshing drink of water in a desert atmosphere. The implications of this study are far more penetrating than anticipated. Whatever ministry God would see fit to permit me to share with Him will not be the same as a result of having sensed the heart of the Puritan divines.

Historians tell us that we should not forget the events of the past so that we can prevent their re-occurrence. Does not the same hold true for that which was successful? If the test of a sermon is the quality of life that it produces, then the Puritans were superbly successful. Thus, we must return to the Puritans and their view of the pulpit if we desire to alter the conduct of those whom we serve. Charles Spurgeon once said, "we shall not adjust our Bible to the age; but before we have done it, by God's grace, we shall adjust the age to the

Bible." In our own country, where literally millions upon millions of people profess a conversion experience—yet unrighteousness is on the increase—we have adjusted the sacred Scripture to the spirit of our age. We must adjust our thinking to that of the Puritans, who held that the primary task of the Church and her ministers was to powerfully preach the Word of God. We can learn much from this devout and courageous group because they were men who did not adjust the biblical role of the minister to their culture, in spite of severe persecution and death.

In order to learn from these great pulpiteers, I read more *of* the Puritans than I did *about* the Puritans; that is, I wanted to discover the hearts of these men more than I wanted to learn facts about them. Consequently, the majority of my research consisted of reading as many Puritan sermons and works as possible. Granted, I did have to wade through the depths of their pedantry and prolixity in their theological works; nevertheless, I was able to accomplish my intent. Not all Puritan sermons are easy to read, but I determined to learn from what they said rather than from what someone else said about them. The rewards of such methodology are too numerous to compare with the alternative system.

All ministry comes from a clear vision of God. Biblical examples would be Isaiah, Ezekiel, Moses, and Paul. In this regard, the Puritan preachers would also be examples, for their ministry in the pulpit was a reflection of how they saw God. Because they saw the sovereign God behind their call to preach, the issue of the infallibility of Scripture was never a concern. God's Word was exactly that; therefore, God would do with it what He intended to do with it: when preached it would accomplish what God intended and create people who would become doers of the Word. The Puritans understood the creative power of God's Word because they saw God creating in and through the Word.

The scope of their ministry in and from the pulpit was dictated and defined by their vision of the holy character of God. The preaching of the Word of God, to the Puritan pastor, was neither a moral homily nor a philosophical essay; it was the authoritative declaration of the will of the blessed God. Therein lay the supreme significance of their preaching ministry. They realized that to the degree they saw God, to that degree their ministries would be effective. As a result, their pulpit ministry did not end at the closing of their sermons. Instead, an entire concept of pastoring, or overseeing the flock, was generated. This ministry of oversight began with themselves.

Since God would use the spoken word to bring about what He desired to accomplish individually and corporately, application or use was of paramount importance. The plain style and methodical construction of their messages reflected this emphasis. So did the pastoral ministry to the flock. The latter was an extension of the former.

The shepherding ministry of the Puritan pastor could be defined as the working out of the proper application of the sermon. Fully aware that the Word proclaimed would cause different conditions upon the soul, the Puritan ministers catechized, counseled, comforted, and communed with their sheep in order to achieve proper and beneficial use of the truths declared by God through their preaching. Their view of the pulpit and its effects moved these men to have a loving concern for their congregations, manifested by an overseeing of individuals long since forgotten in most modern-day ministers. The Puritans' view of the pulpit as the platform for the proclamation of the creative Word of God was the axis on which their lives turned.

As I began this research, I brought into the project two

concerns that may or may not have been well grounded. One has been alleviated; one still remains. The spirit of melancholy that appeared to exist within Puritanism perplexed me. After reading their sermons, and discovering that their pastoral ministry was a continuation of their preaching ministry, I am better able to handle this issue. The Church has rendered too harsh a judgment on our Puritan brethren concerning this issue, in my opinion. Too much emphasis has been given to their political life and not enough to their pastoring life. I now firmly believe that the Puritan preachers were well aware of the depressions caused by their dogmatic expositions, yet this awareness became an asset to their total ministry and not a hindrance as I once presumed. Understanding their concept of the pulpit and the responsibilities related thereto has freed me to appreciate more fully their uniqueness. I will admit that the English Puritans seemed to deal more effectively with this than did their New World counterparts. Is it possible that the spirit of independence was a hindrance in the ministry of the New England Puritans?

Even though my concern for the melancholy spirit of the Puritan era has been assuaged by a better understanding of their pastoral ministry to their flocks, I must admit to a concern that arose the more I read of their weekly activities. I was unable to sense from their sermons and works very much emphasis on "equipping of the saints for the work of service, to the building up of the body of Christ" (Eph. 4:12 NASB). While these men may have been the ones who set the standard for pastoral care and shepherding, did they do all of the shepherding alone? I did discover several examples where the Puritan pastor and elders visited families and catechized, but only in the context of both appearing at the same time. Perhaps the cultural setting may have added to this tendency, but I sensed that the Puritan preacher did most or all of the shepherding alone. The majority of their works on shepherding were directed to their fellow pastors and not to the leaders of their local congregations. The separatism of the clergy within Puritanism may have dictated this style of leadership. I would think that the ministry to a local flock would be greatly deepened by the minister adopting the Puritan concept of shepherding, but directed to, through, and with the elders.

The emphasis of the New Testament is that the local church is led and shepherded by a plurality of elders. Everywhere one turns in the New Testament, the church (singular) has pastors (plural). There is no example in the New Testament of an orderly church having one overseer. The church that has a plurality of undershepherds is the orderly church, not the church that has a single undershepherd (Phil. 1:1; Acts 20:17; Acts 14:23; I Peter 5:1–4). Christ, as the Head of the church, is our one, singular Shepherd; He gives a plurality of undershepherds to share in the oversight of the flock in each local situation.

Combining the Puritan emphasis on the preacher being a shepherd with the New Testament emphasis on a plurality of undershepherds would dictate that one of the major responsibilities of a pastor must be leadership development. Applying what the Puritan preachers did with their flocks to the leaders of a local congregation would be an excellent way to reproduce oneself by equipping leaders in order to shepherd the flock most effectively.

Sensing the Puritan preacher's commitment to his pastoral ministry as an extension of the pulpit ministry gives an excitement in comprehending what properly equipped leaders could do in a local church. Leadership development must be a priority for every pastor.

The other presupposition, the lack of body life, is still unresolved. There does not appear to be much participation on the part of the people, in a corporate sense, in the worship experience. Perhaps the answer lies somewhere in the vastness of the available resources of the Puritans which I have yet to uncover. On the other hand, the lack of body participation in terms of our contemporary society may be one of the pitfalls of the movement.

Perhaps the two concerns can be dealt with simultaneously. By properly equipping the leaders and saints to do the ministry, body life and worship will no longer be left to worship leaders; worship will be an expression of the grateful hearts of people who are participating with God in His ministry to the world. Thus, worship becomes ministry and ministry is an act of worship.

A cursory review of the history of the Church dictates our response to the findings of this project. From Church history we can learn that the most decadent times in a society are those periods when the position of the pulpit has declined. Equally important from history's annals, we can observe what preceeded times of great revival and subsequent righteousness—it was biblical preaching. Preaching the creative Word of God with conviction, clarity, compassion, and consequence has always heralded the periods of divine visitation of the power and presence of God. Great preaching was the means by which God brought about revival. It was also a consequence of revival. What we have in our nation today is "revivalism," or the activity of revival. We do not have a sovereign visitation of the Great Revivalist. We have a flurry of religious activity, but not a proportional amount of accompanying righteousness. We must alter our posture of preaching before God may be pleased to visit us with revival. The Scriptures—most notably the Book of Acts and the Pastoral Epistles—instruct it; the history of the Church supports it; and the Puritans prove it. The change must begin with an altered view of the pulpit. Here we can learn from the great Puritan pulpiteers. For those who are chosen of God to be pastor-teachers and are given to the church as a gift, we must radically adjust the focus and framework of our view of the pulpit. The pulpit must become, as it was to the Puritan pastors before us, the very axis on which our entire life and ministry revolves. Our preaching must crush the rocks of unbelief and disobedience, and smooth out the path so that the paving ministry of overseeing the flock will make the narrow road a reality.

An overriding feature of the ministry of the Puritans that comforted my heart was the realization that only God could do His work.

Despite their exhaustive hours of study, vigorous efforts to shepherd their people consistently, and constant watching of their own condition, the Puritan pastors realized that all their efforts were for naught if God did not graciously work His grace in the lives of people. The ministry was God's and could only be produced by God. To the Puritans, if God did not do the ministry, the ministry would not get done.

This study has confirmed the belief that the proper motivation for ministry is not expected success or fear of failure, but a love response to what God has done to one personally. That was the heart of the Puritan concept of ministry. Motivation was a love response to the mercy and grace of God.

Charles Spurgeon has been described as a Puritan born one hundred years too late. If anyone demonstrated the Puritan mindset of the pulpit after the time of Puritanism, Spurgeon would be the example. He admonishes all pastors to "make no mistake here; we shall not watch our congregation to take our cue from it, but we shall keep our eye on the infallible Word, and preach according to its instructions. Our Master sits on high, and not in the chairs of the scribes and doctors, who regulate the theories of the century." Such was the Puritan view of the pulpit.

We worship the same God the Puritans worshipped; we study the same Bible the Puritans studied—why do we not have the same view of the pulpit?

Bibliography

Periodicals

Packer, J. I. "Puritan Evangelism." The Banner of Truth, 9:4–13, [n.d.].

Ryle, J. C. "Past & Present Ministers Compared." The Banner of Truth, 9:37-38, [n.d.].

Books

Bannerman, James. *The Church of Christ.* Rpt. Carlisle, Pa.: Banner of Truth, 1974.

Baxter, Richard. *The Reformed Pastor.* Rpt. Carlisle, Pa.: Banner of Truth, 1979.

Boston, Thomas. *The Complete Works of Thomas Boston.* 12 vols. Rpt. Wheaton: Richard Owen Roberts, 1980.

Brooks, Thomas. *The Complete Works of Thomas Brooks*, ed. Alexander B. Grosart. 6 vols. Rpt. Carlisle, Pa.: Banner of Truth, 1980.

Bridges, Charles. *The Christian Ministry.* Rpt. Carlisle, Pa.: Banner of Truth, 1980.

Chandos, John. *In God's Name: Examples of Preaching in England 1534-1662.* Indianapolis: Bobbs-Merrill, 1971.

Charnock, Stephen. *Discourses Upon the Existence and Attributes of God.* 3rd ed. Grand Rapids: Baker, 1981.

Dallimore, Arnold A. *George Whitefield*. 2 vols. Wheaton: Cornerstone Books, 1979.

Davies, Horton. *The Worship of the English Puritans*. Morgan, Pa.: Soli Deo Gloria, 1997.

Dowley, Tim., ed. *Eerdmans Handbook to the History of Christianity*. Grand Rapids: Eerdmans, 1978.

Edwards, Jonathan. *The Complete Works of Jonathan Edwards*. Rev. ed. Edward Hickman. 2 vols. Rpt. Carlisle, Pa.: Banner of Truth, 1979.

Flavel, John. *The Works of John Flavel*. 6 vols. 2nd ed. Carlisle, Pa.: Banner of Truth, 1982.

Gerstner, John H. *Jonathan Edwards, Evangelist*. Rpt. Pittsburgh: Soli Deo Gloria, 1995.

Gill, John. *A Body of Divinity*. Rpt. Grand Rapids: Sovereign Grace Books, 1971.

Goodwin, Thomas. *The Complete Works of Thomas Goodwin*. 12 vols. Rpt. Louisville, Miss.: Mounts Publishing, 1979.

Henry, Matthew. *The Complete Works of Matthew Henry*. Vol. I. Rpt. Grand Rapids: Baker, 1978.

Hulse, Erroll., and others. *Preaching Yesterday and Today*. Sussex: Carey Publications, 1972.

Levy, Babette M. *Preaching in the First Half Century of New England History*. New York: Russell & Russell, 1944.

Lewis, Peter. *The Genius of Puritanism*. Morgan, Pa.: Soli Deo Gloria, 1995.

Lloyd-Jones, D. Martyn. *Preaching and Preachers*. 12th ed. Grand Rapids: Zondervan, 1981.

Miller, Perry. *The New England Mind: The Seventeenth Century*. Boston: Beacon Press, 1961.

Nichols, James, editor. *Puritan Sermons 1659-1689*. 6 vols. Rpt. Wheaton: Richard Owens Roberts, 1981.

Owen, John. *The Works of John Owen*, ed. William H. Goold. 16 vols. Rpt. 3rd ed. Carlisle, Pa.: Banner of Truth, 1977.

Schaff, Philip. *History of the Christian Church*. 8 vols. Rpt. Grand Rapids: Eerdmans, 1980.

Sibbes, Richard. *The Works of Richard Sibbes*, ed. Alexander B. Grosart. 7 vols. Rpt. Carlisle, Pa.: Banner of Truth, 1973–1981.

Spurgeon, Charles H. *Lectures To My Students*. 9th ed. Grand Rapids: Zondervan, 1970.

———*An All Round Ministry*. Rpt. 3rd ed. Carlisle, Pa.: Banner of Truth, 1978.

Thomas, I. D. E., comp. ed. *The Golden Treasury of Puritan Quotations*. Carlisle, Pa.: Banner of Truth, 1977.

Toon, Peter. *God's Statesman: The Life and Work of John Owen*. Grand Rapids: Zondervan, 1973.

Tracy, Joseph. *The Great Awakening: A History of the Revival of Religion in the Time of Edwards and Whitefield.* Rpt. Carlisle, Pa.: Banner of Truth, 1976.

Traill, Robert. *The Works of Robert Traill.* 4 vols. Rpt. Carlisle, PA.: Banner of Truth, 1975.

Turnbull, Ralph G. *Jonathan Edwards the Preacher.* Grand Rapids: Baker, 1958.

Watson, Thomas. *Body of Divinity.* Rpt. Grand Rapids: Baker, 1979.

Webber, F. R. *A History of Preaching in Britain and America.* Milwaukee: Northwestern Publishing House, 1952.

The
Focus of
the Gospel
in
Puritan
Preaching

Preface

Since the Reformation, Protestant Christendom has developed two concepts and two styles of evangelism. One may label them the "Puritan" type and the "modern" type. The Church is so accustomed to the modern style that it scarcely recognizes the other as evangelism at all; at a minimum many consider it to be unloving and unaggressive. Both are characterized by identifiable methods emanating from a recognizable message.

How one thinks determines how one acts; thus one's methodology of evangelism is shaped by how one perceives the content of the gospel message. Nowhere is this more obvious than in comparing these two historical styles. In order to fully grasp the different concepts and styles, I have set forth by way of contrast the content of the message of Puritan evangelism with that of the modern type, which was popularized, if not invented, by Charles G. Finney in the 1820s.

The content of the gospel is an issue of major importance for the present age. If Finney's view of the message of the gospel, specifically his doctrine of the natural state of man, is correct, then the modified and adapted methods of modern Finneyism must be judged as right also. But if his view of man is wrong, then his new measures, which characterize most modern evangelism, must be judged as inappropriate and, indeed, detrimental to the real work of biblical evangelism. If Finney's doctrine is rejected, then his methods, as the reader will see, must be judged as disastrous.

Motivation for this study is twofold. First, one called to be a herald of the *kerygma*—message or preaching—of God (1 Corinthians 1:21) must recognize the limitations of the

83

content of the message, just as Micaiah understood his responsibilities when speaking to Ahab, "As surely as the Lord lives, I can tell him only what my God says" (2 Chronicles 18:13). Preachers are charged with preaching a message already given, not creating one. The preacher is not called and sent by God to make a quick sale but to deliver a message. What, then, is the message?

Second, in the first part of this work (on the Puritan view of the pulpit) we gleaned from the heart of the Puritan divines their methodology. In the evening of the Puritan age, Robert Traill almost repeated the very words of William Perkins spoken at the dawning of Elizabethan Puritanism. Traill said, "The principal work of a minister is preaching, and the principal benefit people have by them is to hear the Lord's Word preached to them." To the Puritans the message *was* the method. Again, then, what was their message?

The majority of this study is centered upon the content of the Puritan message because of its nearly forgotten impact upon the lives of the converted. In this age of revivalism one does not see the fruit of revival—increasing righteousness—that one observed in the Puritan era.

Chapter 1

Introduction

In the August 1980 issue of *Moody Monthly*, Robert Flood reported the findings of a religious survey of a cross-section of the American people. The poll, conducted by George Gallup, Jr., revealed the following:

1. One out of five adults over 18—approximately 31 million—claim to be evangelical.

2. Eight out of ten American evangelicals claim to have had a life-changing experience through Christianity.

3. Fifty million Americans claim to have had a personal experience with Jesus Christ.

4. Over 39 million Americans claim to have invited Christ into their lives.

5. Sixty-nine million Americans over the age of 18 hope to go to heaven because of their faith.

6. Fifty percent of American Protestant teenagers claim a born-again experience.

7. Sixty-five million adults believe the Bible to be the Word of God.

8. Forty million adults are regular church attenders.

The Gallup Poll concluded that Jesus Christ has never been more popular than today.[1] Yet consider the information reported from a CBS News study: the prime location for the committing of a violent crime is the home. This report also

---

[1] Robert Flood, "What the Gallup Poll Says to Evangelicals," *Moody Monthly*, August 1980, pp. 22–27.

revealed that every two minutes there is a teenage pregnancy and that within the next thirty minutes 28 teenagers will attempt suicide, 685 teenagers will try narcotics, and 188 teenagers will experience a serious drinking problem.

Why the contrast? Why, if Jesus Christ is more popular today than in any time in our nation's history, does the church lack power and wield so little influence in society? Why do the 65 million believers in the Bible reported by the Gallup Poll have a divorce rate of over sixty percent? As we approach a new millennium, research conducted by such observers as George Barna and James Hunter demonstrate an increasing disparity between claim and conduct in modern evangelism revealed in the previous decade. Not much has changed. Based on the evidence, one must cry out in exasperation, "Where are these believers, and where is the proof?"

The Scriptures teach that a true child of God is committed to righteousness as a result of what God has done. Paul writes, "For God did not call us to be impure, but to live a holy life" (1 Thess. 4:7). Peter affirms the changed life by stating, "As obedient children, do not conform to the evil desires you had when you lived in ignorance" (1 Peter 1:14).

Church history teaches us that the church is always drifting away from the Scriptures; therefore, we are in need of frequent self-examination. If one compares the evangelistic efforts of men greatly used in evangelism—Bunyan, Whitefield, Edwards, Spurgeon, and the majority of the Puritans—with present-day evangelism, one will notice the disparity in message and methods. One will also discover a wide variance in what was accomplished in the life of the supposedly converted. I wish only to compare the message of the Puritans with what is offered today. From the message flows the means to achieve what one holds to be the end in view in the proclamation of the gospel.

The intent of this work is to discover the focus of the gospel message—God or man—by contrasting the two styles. Original works from both periods were considered. Rather than presenting historical facts about the Puritans, this author chose to let the Puritan evangelists speak for themselves through their sermons and period literature. The same courtesy was offered the modern evangelists. Evangelical hand-pieces or tracts presently used were compared for content of the message in the following areas: God and His holiness, man and his sinfulness, the person and work of Christ, repentance and faith, and the end in view, or response anticipated by the message. Present-day books on methods of evangelism generally used in training sessions were examined for message focus. Following the tradition of the great Puritan preachers, a series of uses is presented to enhance application of the results uncovered. At the end of this book, a comparative overview of the plan of salvation of the two periods is offered as a summary.

In order to put this study in proper context, one must begin with a basic characterization of evangelism of this modern age; evangelism of the Puritan age will be easily realized by the material presented.

Modern evangelism adopts a twofold concept of life in the local church: an alternating cycle of converting and edifying. As a result, evangelism is often a scheduled activity that takes on the guise of a periodic recruiting campaign. Many times these scheduled events are additional and auxiliary to the normal ministry of the local congregation. Special gatherings are arranged and special speakers are often secured to conduct these meetings. The aim, the end in view, of the meeting is directed to obtaining from the unconverted an immediate, conscious, decisive act of faith in Christ as

Savior. At the close of the meeting, opportunity is given to those who wish to respond to come to the front, raise a hand, or perform some other mechanism of public display as a means of indicating their decision to accept Christ. Leighton Ford addressed the importance of this feature of modern evangelism by stating:

> I am convinced that the giving of some kind of public invitation to come to Christ is not only theologically correct, but also emotionally sound. Men need this opportunity for expression. The inner decision for Christ is like driving a nail through a board. The open declaration of it is like clinching the nail on the other side, so that it is not easily pulled out. Impression without expression can lead to depression.[2]

Since the consent of man's will is the main objective to be gained, modern evangelism presupposes that a response which involves public action will commit people's wills more surely than if they were left to seek Christ in private. Thus the modernists link the theological with the psychological and represent the necessity of the appeal to come forward as "a means of obeying Christ's command to confess Him before men, and a step which will help him to make the decision definite and clear-cut."[3] Modern evangelism makes a close association between the operations of the Spirit and the actual events of the scheduled meeting; thus, to fail to provide an opportunity to decide for Christ at the right time could result in the possible loss of souls who might relapse into their former state of indecision. The assumption is that

---

2 Leighton Ford, *The Christian Persuader* (New York: MacMillan, 1966), p. 124.
3 *Ibid.*

the more public the response, the less likely the relapse. Counselors are then instructed to query the person as to the nature of their intention, and to assure them after some discussion of their salvation because of what they have done— invited Christ into their life. The final act in modern evangelism is the drafting of these new converts into the life of the local church.

The basis for such tradition is found in the writings and practical methods of Charles G. Finney. In the 1820s, Finney introduced what he called the protracted meeting— our present-day evangelistic campaign. In addition, he provided a pew in the front where individuals could come to be spoken to as a group or individually; this was known as "the anxious seat." Finney was known to say at the end of a sermon, "There is the anxious seat; come out, and avow determination to be on the Lord's side."[4]

One may say that the results justify the methods, but that statement presupposes that the same results are achieved by different concepts and styles of evangelism. Is an immediate response to the message of the gospel the basis for evaluation? An internal cleansing of the heart whereby God gives a new heart and puts within a new Spirit is a more biblical evaluation. Here God removes the heart of stone and gives a heart of flesh that has within it His Spirit, which causes the person to follow His decrees and be careful to keep His laws (Ezek. 36:26–27). Should not this be the biblical barometer for evaluation? This may or may not be immediate, and certainly requires some time to be accurately recognized.

Based on the lack of biblical evidence in the altered conduct of many who profess Christ, this writer would suggest

---

[4] Charles G. Finney, *Revival Lectures* (Broadview, Il.: Cicero Bible Press, n.d.), p. 304.

that there are many who profess Christ but do not possess Christ. A comparison of the tests and traits of a possessor of saving faith as written in 1 John with the conduct of the modern professor would suggest that the methods based on the message of today's evangelism have a natural tendency to produce a crop of false converts. "The truth is that the majority of Finney's converts fell away, and so, it seems, have the majority of those since Finney's day whose decision has been secured by the use of such methods."[5] In reality, the methods of Finneyism do not work when results are honestly exposed to the biblical standard. The modern trend is not to expect more than a small percentage of converts to survive.[6] The Puritan type of evangelism, as presented in this book, was the consistent expression in message and method of their deep conviction that the conversion of a sinner is a gracious sovereign work of Divine power. J. I. Packer, in his "Introduction" to John Owen's *The Death of Death in the Death of Christ*, clearly contrasted the two styles of evangelism:

> There is no doubt that Evangelism today is in a state of perplexity and unsettlement. . . . Without realizing it we have during the past century bartered the gospel (the biblical gospel) for a substitute product which, though it looks similar enough in points of detail, is as a whole a decidedly different thing. Hence our troubles; for the substitute product does not answer the ends for which the authentic gospel has in past days proved itself so mighty. The new gospel conspicuously fails to produce deep reverence, deep repentance, deep humil-

---

[5] J. I. Packer, "Puritan Evangelism," *The Banner of Truth*
[6] Personal interview with former Campus Crusade director, University of Missouri, April 1981. Only 3 out of 12 converts were expected not to fall away.

ity, a spirit of worship, a concern for the church. Why? We would suggest that the reason lies in its own character in content. It fails to make men God-centered in their thoughts and God-fearing in their hearts because this is not primarily what it is trying to do. One way of stating the difference between it and the old gospel is to say that it is too exclusively concerned to be "helpful" to man—to bring peace, comfort, happiness, satisfaction—and too little concerned to glorify God. The old gospel is "helpful" too—more so, indeed, than is the new—but (so to speak) incidentally, for its first concern was always to give glory to God. It was always and essentially a proclamation of divine sovereignty in mercy and judgment, a summons to bow down and worship the mighty Lord on whom man depends for all good, both in nature and in grace. Its center of reference was unambiguously God. But in the new gospel the center of reference is man. This is just to say that the old gospel was religious in a way that the new is not. Whereas the chief aim of the old was to teach men to worship God, the concern of the new seems limited to making them feel better. The subject of the old gospel was God and His ways with men; the subject of the new is man and the help God gives him. There is a world of difference. The whole perspective and emphasis of gospel preaching has changed.[7]

Continuing his evaluation, Packer concluded:

From this change of interest has sprung a change of content, for the new gospel has in effect reformulated the biblical message in supposed interest of "helpfulness." Accordingly, the thesis of man's natural inability to believe, of God's free election being the ultimate cause of salvation, and of Christ's dying specifically for

---

[7] J. I. Packer, "Introduction" to John Owen's *The Death of Death in the Death of Christ* (rpt. Carlisle, Pa.: Banner of Truth, 1983), pp. 1–2.

His sheep are not preached. These doctrines, it would be said, are not "helpful"; they would drive sinners to despair by suggesting to them that it is not in their power to be saved through Christ. . . . The result of these omissions is that part of the biblical gospel is now preached as if it were the whole of the gospel, and a half-truth masquerading as the whole becomes a complete untruth. Thus, we appeal to men as if they all had the ability to receive Christ at any time; we speak of His redeeming work as if He had done no more by dying than making it possible for us to save ourselves by believing; we speak of God's love as if it were no more than the general willingness to receive any who will turn and trust; and we depict the Father and the Son, not as sovereignly acting and drawing sinners to themselves, but as waiting in quiet impotence "at the door of our hearts" for us to let them in. It is undeniable that this is how we preach; perhaps this is what we really believe. But it needs to be said that this set of twisted half-truths is something other than the biblical gospel. The Bible is against us when we preach in this way; and the fact that such preaching has become almost standard practice among us only shows how urgent it is that we should review this matter. To recover the old, authentic, biblical gospel, and to bring our preaching and practice back into line with it, is perhaps our most pressing need.[8]

The issue with which one is confronted by this study of the focus of the gospel in Puritan preaching is obvious. Which road are we to take in our endeavors to spread the gospel to every creature? Shall we progress along the highway of modern Finneyism, the intensive mass-scale, short-term campaign, with its pressing for decisions and its quick follow-the-numbers handling of all new converts with the

---

[8] Packer, "Introduction", p. 2.

same machinery? Or do we return back to the old path of the Puritan divines, the quieter, broader-based, long-term strategy based on the local church? As a preacher, a herald of the biblical gospel, is one called to wage a battle of wills between oneself and one's hearers, with the end in view of bringing them to the breaking point? Should not we be steadfast in delivering God's message, leaving it to the sovereign Spirit to draw men to faith through the power of the message in His own way and at His own speed? Is the evaluation to be an external response to a time-limited opportunity, or the perseverance of the newly reborn creature in the pursuit of righteousness? Which is loyal to the *kerygma* of God? Which glorifies God? These are the questions that prompted this study, and which demand our most urgent consideration.

Chapter 2

The View of God

The basis of evangelism in Puritan preaching was a vigorous biblical theism. When examining the period literature, one will discover a common thread in all their expositions. The Puritans preached a vigorous doctrine of God.

Modern evangelism would say that the most important verse in the Bible is John 3:16: "And God so loved . . . ." The Puritan evangelists would unequivocally say it was Genesis 1:1: "In the beginning God. . . ." Anything that happened from creation on was a result of the unfolding of what the Creator God was doing to accomplish the ends that He designed for His own glory. They knew that the concepts of atonement, reconciliation, forgiveness, and justification had absolutely no biblical meaning apart from some basic understanding of the God of the Bible who does justify, who does effect the reconciliation, and who does draw sinners to Himself. The Puritans made no assumption that people knew the God of John 3:16. Thus, their evangel began with the proclamation of the doctrine of God.

In a chapter entitled "The Miseries of the Unconverted" found in Joseph Alleine's *An Alarm to the Unconverted*, the author expounded in vivid detail how every attribute of God is against the sinner in his impenitent state. His holiness, His justice, His faithfulness, and His purity are directed against him until the sinner is prepared, as the Spirit of God takes that truth and makes it real to him. Then, and only then, would the sinner be in the condition to receive as good

news the fact that the same God, whose attributes burn
against him in righteous indignation, has provided a way of
mercy and escape in His Son, Jesus Christ the Lord. Alleine
stated:

> His face is against you. "The face of the Lord is against
> them that do evil, to cut off the remembrance of
> them" (Psalm 34:16). Woe unto them whom God shall
> set His face against. . . . His heart is against you. He
> hates all the workers of iniquity. Man, does not your
> heart tremble to think of your being an object of God's
> hatred? All His attributes are against you. His justice is
> like a flaming sword unsheathed against you. The holi-
> ness of God is against you. He is not only angry with
> you—so He may be with His children—but He has a
> fixed habitual displeasure against you. God's nature is
> contrary to sin, and so He cannot delight in a sinner out
> of Christ.[1]

The Reverend Thomas Lye, in a sermon entitled, "How
Are We to Live by Faith on Divine Providence?", spoke of
the nature of trust in God: "The grand reason why God is so
little trusted is because He is so little known."[2] Knowledge
of God is of such necessity to a right trust that it is put as a
synonym for trust. The knowledge of God was paramount in
the preaching of the Puritans; also the function of Scripture
as the revealer of God was clearly pronounced. In answer to
the question, "What do the Scriptures principally teach?",
John Flavel, citing question 3 of the *Westminster Shorter*

---

[1] Joseph Alleine, *An Alarm to the Unconverted* (1671; rpt. Carlisle, Pa.:
Banner of Truth, 1978), pp. 80–99.
[2] Thomas Lye, "How Are We to Live by Faith on Divine Providence?",
in *Puritan Sermons 1659–1689*, translator James Nichols (rpt. Wheaton:
Richard Owen Roberts, 1981), I:371.

Catechism, succinctly stated the Puritan position that "The scriptures principally teach what man is to believe concerning God, and what duty God requires of man."[3]

The joining of the person of God and the responsibility of man characterized the Puritan message. After a series of questions concerning the nature and characteristics of God, Flavel made application of the doctrines in the form of a question in his explanation of the Catechism:

> Q.4. What is the first lesson to be learnt from God's infinity?
> A. That therefore men should tremble even in secret.[4]

Man's personal responsibility to God as the infinite Creator was seen as intricately linked to the nature of God. The Puritan divines preached that man was personally responsible to God because man was made in the image of His person.

In the Puritan mind, man's response to sin was in direct proportion to his understanding of the holiness of God. Matthew Henry stated, "No attribute of God is more dreadful to sinners than his holiness."[5]

The doctrine of God permeated Puritan expositions, even in subjects not dealing with the person of God directly. In a discourse dealing with "Precious Remedies Against Satan's Devices," Thomas Brooks listed the first remedy:

---

[3] John Flavel, *The Works of John Flavel* (Carlisle, Pa.: Banner of Truth, 1982), VI:144.

[4] Flavel, VI:147.

[5] John Blanchard, *Gathered Gold* (Hertfordshire, England: Evangelical Press, 1984), p. 117.

The first remedy against this device of Satan is, to have your hearts strongly affected with the greatness, holiness, majesty, and glory of that God before whom you stand, and with whom your souls do converse in religious services.

Ah! when men have poor, low, light, slight thoughts of God, in their drawing near to God they tempt the devil to bestir himself, and to cast in a multitude of vain thoughts to disturb and distract the soul in its waiting on God. There is nothing that will contribute so much to the keeping out of vain thoughts as to look upon God as an omniscient God, an omnipresent God, an omnipotent God, a God full of all glorious perfections, a God whose majesty, purity, and glory will not suffer him to behold the least iniquity.[6]

Brooks concluded this line of reasoning by stating that "the reason why the blessed saints and glorious angels in heaven have not so much as one vain thought is, because they are greatly affected with the greatness, holiness, majesty, purity, and glory of God." Even when these powerful proclaimers of the doctrines of God were addressing believers, they clearly espoused the person of God as the basis of one's responsibility. In offering a fifth defense against Satan, Brooks admonished:

The fifth remedy against this device of Satan is, to labour more and more to be filled with the fulness of God, and to be enriched with all spiritual and heavenly things. . . . Take it for an experienced truth, the more the soul is filled with the fulness of God and enriched with spiritual and heavenly things, the less room there

---

6 Thomas Brooks, *The Complete Works of Thomas Brooks* (1861; rpt. Carlisle, Pa.: Banner of Truth, 1980), VI:86.

is in that soul for vain thoughts. The fuller the vessel is of wine, the less room there is for water. Oh, then, lay up much of God.[7]

The Puritans were masters of discriminating application. In a sermon entitled, "The Mute Christian Under the Smarting Rod," Brooks applied the doctrines of God to the conscience of his audience, not taking for granted that they all were in Christ. Brooks charged:

> Aaron had an eye to the sovereignty of God, and that silences him. And Job had an eye upon the majesty of God, and that stills him. And Eli had an eye upon the authority and presence of God, and that quiets him. A man never comes to humble himself, nor to be silent under the mighty hand of God, until he comes to see the hand of God as a mighty hand. I Peter 5:6: "Humble yourselves therefore under the mighty hand of God." When men look upon the hand of God as a weak hand, a feeble hand, a low hand, a mean hand, their hearts rise against His hand.[8]

With such a multiplicity of emphasis on biblical theism, the sovereignty of God became a hallmark in their preaching. In a message pleading with sinners to come to Christ in faith, Thomas Brooks described the power of God: "The sovereignty of God is that golden sceptre in His hand by which He will make all bow, either by His word or by His works, by His mercies or by His judgments."[9] Stephen Charnock declared, "To be God and sovereign are insepara-

---

[7] Brooks, VI:89.
[8] Brooks, VI:299.
[9] *Gathered Gold*, p. 124.

ble."[10] Charles Spurgeon, a latter-day Puritan as evidenced
by the doctrines he preached, sounded the sovereignty of
God in clear tones. Spurgeon declared to believers that
"whether you shall live to reach home today or not depends
absolutely upon God's will."[11]

In another sermon addressed to sinners, Spurgeon heralded this explanation of the sovereignty of God while using
as his text 2 Cor. 5:21:

> The God of Scripture is a sovereign God; that is, He is a
> God who has absolute authority, and absolute power to
> do exactly as He pleaseth. Over the head of God there is
> no law, upon His arm there is no necessity; He knoweth
> no rule but His own free and mighty will. And although
> He cannot be unjust, and cannot do anything but good,
> yet in His nature is absolutely free; for goodness is the
> freedom of God's nature.[12]

In making application to salvation, Spurgeon continued:

> God is not to be controlled by the will of man, not the
> desires of man, not by fate in which the superstitious
> believe; He is God, doing as He willeth in the armies of
> heaven, and in this lower world. He is God, too, who
> giveth no account of his matters; he makes his creatures
> just what he chooses to make them, and does with them
> just as he will. . . . He is the God of predestination; the
> God upon whose absolute will the hinge of fate doth
> turn."[13]

---

[10] *Ibid.*
[11] *Ibid.*
[12] Charles Spurgeon, *The New Park Street Pulpit and Metropolitan Tabernacle Pulpit Sermons*, 1855–1917 (rpt. Pasadena, Tex.: Pilgrim Publications, 1981), III:274.
[13] Spurgeon, III:275.

In applying the truth of God to the reasoning process of the sinner, the Puritans would never condescend to proclaim that man had a choice in controlling the operations of a sovereign God. Spurgeon, in the same sermon, continued: "This is the God of the Bible, this is the God whom we adore; no weak, pusillanimous God, who is controlled by the will of men, who cannot steer the bark of providence, but a God unalterable, infinite, unerring."[14] Thus, their view of God determined their view of the salvation process. The Puritan believed and preached that no sinner was ever saved by giving his heart to God, but by God giving His heart to the sinner. Salvation was a majestic display of the grace of God because the Puritans viewed it as a work of God. Thomas Hooker declared that "the almighty power of God in the conversion of a sinner is the most mysterious of all the works of God."[15] The term the Puritans used to describe God's involvement in bringing sinners to Himself was "effectual calling," "calling" being the scriptural word used to describe the process in Romans 8:30, 2 Thess. 2:14, 2 Tim. 1:9, and elsewhere, and the adjective "effectual" being added to distinguish it from the ineffectual or general call mentioned in Matt. 20:16 and 22:14–18.

Because they saw God as a holy God who alone could meet the demands of His own nature, the Puritans preached that only God could effect the calling, and He did so at His own pleasure. The Puritans loved to dwell on the scriptural thought of God's Divine power put forth in effectual calling. While they generally taught that a normal conversion was not commonly a spectacular affair, they did give leeway to the fact that it could be. In either case, these preachers saw how

---

[14] *Gathered Gold*, p. 51.
[15] *Banner of Truth*, Feb. 1980, Issue 97, p. 12.

great an exercise of God's power every man's effectual calling
involved. Thomas Goodwin observed:

> In the calling of some there shoots up very suddenly an
> election-conversion (I use to call it so). You shall, as it
> were, see election take hold of a man, pull him out with
> a mighty power, stamp upon him the divine nature, stub
> up corrupt nature by the roots, root up self-love, put in
> a principle of love to God, and launch him forth a new
> creature the first day. . . . He did so with Paul, and it is
> not without example in others after him.
>
> The works are visible tokens of election by such a work
> of calling, as all the powers in heaven and earth could
> not have wrought upon a man's soul so, nor changed a
> man so of a sudden, but only that divine power that cre-
> ated the world (and) raised Christ from the dead.[17]

John Owen, as well as his peers, saw effectual calling as
the unfolding mercy of God as Creator, with man being the
recipient of what God chose to do. He expounded this in a
sermon on Acts 16:9 as "a vision of unchangeable, free mercy
in sending the means of grace to undeserving sinners."[18]
Owen first stated this principle and then followed with an
illustration:

> All events and effects, especially concerning the propa-
> gation of the gospel, and the Church of Christ, are in
> their greatest variety regulated by the eternal purpose
> and counsel of God. Some are sent the gospel, some not.
> In this chapter . . . the gospel is forbidden to be

---

[17] Thomas Goodwin, *The Complete Works of Thomas Goodwin* (Edinburgh:
James Nichols, 1863–65), IX:279.
[18] John Owen, *The Works of John Owen* (rpt. Carlisle, Pa.: Banner of
Truth, 1977), XV:1.

> preached in Asia or Bithynia; which restraint, the Lord
> by His providence as yet continueth to many parts of
> the world; while to some nations the gospel is sent . . .
> as in my text, Macedonia.[19]

Then, to press home the application, Owen asked why
some people hear and some people do not, and, when it is
heard, why are there "various effects, some continuing in
impenitence, others in sincerity closing with Jesus Christ?"
He answered:

> In effectual working of grace . . . when do you think it
> takes its rule and determination . . . that it should be di-
> rected to John, not Judas; Simon Peter, not Simon
> Magus? Why only from this discriminating counsel of
> God from eternity . . . Acts 13:48. . . . The purpose of
> God's election, is the rule of dispensing saving grace.[20]

The great evangelist, Jonathan Edwards, often stressed
the same point. In a message representative of the
Edwardsian emphasis on the character of God from Romans
9:18, the evangelist defined sovereignty as "His absolute
right of disposing of all creatures according to His own pleasure."[21] In this message, Edwards listed various manners in
which God's sovereignty is displayed in the dispensations of
grace. After listing several advantages bestowed upon persons, Edwards wrote:

> In bestowing salvation on some who had few advantages.
> . . . In calling some to salvation, who have been

---

[19] *Ibid*, p. 1.

[20] *Ibid*.

[21] Jonathan Edwards, *The Complete Works of Jonathan Edwards* (rpt.
Carlisle, Pa.: Banner of Truth, 1979), II:849.

heinously wicked, and leaving others, who have been
very moral and religious persons. . . . In saving some of
those who seek salvation and not others (i.e., bringing
some convicted sinners to saving faith while others
never attain to sincerity).[22]

The Puritans maintained that this display of the
sovereignty of God was glorious. Edwards declared, "It is
part of the glory of God's mercy that it is sovereign
mercy."[23] No preacher in the Puritan tradition emphasized
the sovereignty of God as frequently or as powerfully as did
Edwards. Much to the surprise of modern readers, his
preaching was evangelistically very fruitful. In his own
words, Edwards described the revival that swept through
his church with this comment:

I think I have found that no discourses have been more
remarkably blessed than those in which the doctrine of
God's absolute sovereignty, with regard to the salvation
of sinners, and his just liberty, with regard to answering
prayer, and succeeding the pains, of natural men, continuing such, have been insisted on.[24]

The basis of the evangelistic message of the Puritans was
the person and character of a holy God. Their evangel started
with God and was pressed home to man. Man's need could
not be discerned apart from some understanding of the character of God. Modern evangelism is the antithesis of such an
emphasis.

In recent years, "The Four Spiritual Laws" has been
widely used as an evangelical handpiece. Produced and dis-

---

22 *Ibid*, II:849.
23 *Ibid*, II:849.
24 *Ibid*, I:353.

tributed by Campus Crusade for Christ, this tract may be
considered representative of the modern mind on evangelism. The tract begins with Law One: "God loves you and
has a wonderful plan for your life." The focus is that God
has something to give you. Man's receiving, not God's be-
stowing, is paramount in this presentation. Sin is addressed
in Law Two, but merely treated as separation from God.

The modern evangel appears to have as its theme the reception of heaven rather than the glory of God. Dr. D. James
Kennedy's *Evangelism Explosion* is a very practical manual for
the training of lay persons in evangelism. In chapters dealing
with both a brief and a more extended presentation of the
gospel, the author suggested several questions to prompt the
discussion into a spiritual direction. The two questions were
as follows:

Question 1: Have you ever come to a place in your
spiritual life where you can say you know for certain that if
you were to die today you would go to heaven?

Question 2: Suppose that you were to die today and
stand before God and He were to say to you, "Why should I
let you into My heaven?" what would you say?[25]

Both are good questions; however, the explanation of the
treatment of those questions centers on the offer of heaven
rather than the majesty of God and His character, and His
demands that His nature not be violated. While the author
does deal with man's inability to earn his salvation and God's
necessity to punish all sin, the emphasis is on what man
receives rather than the fact that God is offended in His
character and nature apart from the person and work of

---

[25] D. James Kennedy, *Evangelism Explosion* (Wheaton: Tyndale, 1973),
p. 22.

Christ.[26] In dealing with the holiness of God and the love of God, Kennedy stated, "The teachings that God emphasizes about Himself are: He is holy and just and must punish sin; but He is so loving and merciful and does not want to punish us. In effect, this created a problem for God which He solved in Jesus Christ."[27]

The Puritan pastor would be appalled with such a statement that God was forced to deal with man on the basis that sin was His problem. Stephen Charnock wrote:

> The whole design of God's love in the death of His Son is to reinstate us in a resemblance to this Divine perfection: whereby He shows what an affection He hath to this excellency of His nature, and what a detestation He hath of evil.[28]

The plan of redemption to the Puritans was a result of what God chose to do in the depths of the counsel of His own will, and not something that He was forced to do because of a benefit to sinful man. They viewed every act as an expression of the glory of God. Charnock stated that "as the creation was erected by Him for His glory, so all the acts of His government are designed for the same end."[29] God was the reason for salvation, not man; man received the overflow of what God was pleased to do to put His glory on display. In 1623, William Gouge preached that "God's glory is the most principal and supreme end of all. As at the next (but subordinate) end, God in His Providence aimeth at His

---

[26] Kennedy, pp. 22–25.

[27] Kennedy, p. 41.

[28] Stephen Charnock, *Discourses Upon the Existence and Attributes of God* (1853, rpt. Grand Rapids: Baker, 1981), II:137.

[29] Charnock, II:140.

children's good."[30]

Puritan preaching contained a theism that directed sinners to God and did not, as modern evangelism does, create an impression that God is waiting to give the sinner something. Puritan preaching was evangelical preaching because their evangel portrayed the infinite chasm between the condition of man and the character of God. For man to be reconciled to God, man would have to come to embrace his spiritual bankruptcy and unworthiness before God. To accomplish this attitude, the Puritans preached a glorious picture of the majesty of a holy God; to do otherwise would have rendered their message powerless and fruitless and doomed man in his hopeless state without God. The Puritans, as evidenced in the words of Stephen Charnock, preached a vigorous biblical theism because they believed that "the creature must be stripped of his unrighteousness, or God of His purity, before they can come together."[31] God was the subject of the gospel, not man.

---

[30] William Gouge, *The Whole Armour of God* (London: John Beale, 1619), p. 32.
[31] Charnock, II:145.

Chapter 3

The View of Man

The reason the Puritans magnified the person of God in the work of quickening the sinner was that they took so seriously the biblical teaching that man was dead in trespasses and sins (Eph. 2:1). These men, whose creed was *Sola Scriptura*, understood this passage to mean that man was radically depraved and sin's helpless bondslave. Nothing other than the quickening power of God could alter that state. Sin held such a strength that only Omnipotence could break its bond; only the Creator of life could raise the dead. In a sermon entitled, "Of the Resurrection," Edmund Calamy preached:

> By nature we have dead souls, dead in sins and trespasses, void of spiritual life; as perfectly under the power of sin, as a dead man is under the power of death; and as unable to do anything that is spiritually good, as a dead man is to do any work. Now a dead soul in sin shall be damned for sin.[1]

Thomas Manton stated, in a sermon on "Man's Impotency To Help Himself Out of That Misery," that "Man, fallen, is destitute of all power and means of rising again, or helping himself out of that misery into which he hath plunged him-

---

[1] Edmund Calamy, "Of the Resurrection," in *Puritan Sermons 1659-1689*, editor James Nichols (rpt. Wheaton: Richard Owen Roberts, 1981), V:457.

self by sin."² Further into the same sermon, Manton explained in vivid detail the Puritan view of man:

> The scripture sets forth man's condition thus: that he is born in sin; (Psalm 51:5) and things natural are not easily altered. Greedy of sin: "He drinketh-in iniquity like water:" (Job 15:6:) it noteth a vehement propension; as greedy to sin, as a thirsty man to drink. Thirst is the most implacable appetite; hunger is far better born. . . . "Every imagination of the thoughts of his heart is" evil, "only evil," and that "continually" (Gen. 6:5). By how many aggravating and increasing circumstances is man's sin there set forth! There is in him a mint always at work: his mind coining evil thoughts, his heart, evil desires and carnal motions; and his memory is the closet and storehouse wherein they are kept.³

After lengthy details in elaborating man's state by nature, Manton concluded this portion of the sermon:

> As weak and "without strength," here in the text; yea stark "dead in trespasses and sins; (Eph. 2:1, 5) yea, worse than dead: a dead man doth no more hurt, his evil dieth with him; but there is a life of resistance and rebellion against God that goes along with this death in sin. Now put all this together, and you may spell out man's misery, what a wretched, impotent creature he is in his natural state. The scripture does not speak this by glances or short touches; neither is it a hyperbole used once or twice but every where, where it professedly speaks of this matter. Certainly, man, contributeth little to his own conversion: he cannot "hunger and

---

² Thomas Manton, "Man's Impotency To Help Himself Out of That Misery," in *Puritan Sermons 1659-1689*.
³ Manton, p. 160.

thirst" after Christ, that "drinks in iniquity like water:" there is nothing in nature to carry him to grace, who is altogether sinful. If the scripture had only said that man had accustomed himself to sin, and was not "born in sin;" that man were somewhat prone to iniquity, and not "greedy" of it; and did often think evil, and not "continually"; that man were somewhat obstinate, and not a "stone," an "adamant"; if the scripture had only said that man were indifferent to God, and not a professed "enemy"; if a captive of sin, and not a "servant"; if only weak, and not "dead"; if only a neuter, and not a "rebel"; then there might be something in man, and the work of conversion not so difficult But the scripture saith the quite contrary.[4]

Manton then proceeded to list several assertions that further proved man's deadness and inability to do anything that is spiritually good. The great Puritan divine polemically summarized, "Well, then. When man can neither know, nor believe, nor obey, nor think, nor speak, nor do anything without grace, surely man is 'without strength,' wholly impotent and unable to turn himself to God."[5]

The Puritan mindset held that sin was such a great force that it was a bond which prevented man from doing anything that would please God, let alone freely seek God. Thomas Brooks spoke to the power of bondage that sin held upon man:

For as bonds tie things together, so doth sin tie the sinner and the curse together. It binds the sinner and wrath together, it links the sinner and hell together: "I perceive that thou art in the gall of bitterness, and in the bond of iniquity," Acts 8:23. Iniquity is a chain, a

---

[4] Manton, p. 161.
[5] Manton, p. 163.

> bond. Now, bonds and chains gall the body, and so doth
> sin the soul; and as poor captives are held fast in their
> chains, so are sinners in their sins; they cannot redeem
> themselves by price, not by power, 2 Tim. 2:26.[6]

This mindset was featured in the instructions given to
men who were preachers of the gospel during the Puritan
era. George Whitefield delivered a sermonic instruction to a
group of fellow clergymen exhorting them in their duties. In
a sermon appropriately titled, "The Duty of a Gospel
Minister," delivered on September 12th, 1741, Whitefield
charged his brethren to preach a biblical gospel. Preaching
from Luke 4:18–19, Whitefield said:

> I take the gospel here, more particularly, as signifying
> the comforts of the gospel; and, therefore, though we
> are to preach Christ Jesus to all freely, to all indefi-
> nitely, yet people will never accept of Him, and we can
> give them no comfort, until that we find they are made
> sick of sin, and made willing to embrace an offered
> Jesus.[7]

Describing the condition of the people as depicted in the
text that are to be preached to, the mighty Whitefield said:

> But by the poor, you are to understand the poor in
> spirit; those who feel their poverty, who bewail their
> misery, those who feel they are lost and undone on ac-
> count of their original and actual sin, and on account of
> the deficiency of their own righteousness. They find

---

[6] Thomas Brooks, *The Complete Works of Thomas Brooks* (1861; rpt.
Carlisle, Pa.: Banner of Truth, 1980), I:86.

[7] George Whitefield, "The Duty of a Gospel Minister" in *The Revivals
of the Eighteenth Century* (1847; rpt. Wheaton: Richard Owen Roberts,
1980), p. 9.

they must accept of salvation, or be damned of God forevermore; they find they have nothing to buy salvation with—they must be entirely beholden of God for it. . . . The next persons are the brokenhearted. . . . Our hearts, by nature, are harder than the nether millstone: they are so hard, that none but God can break them. . . . Well, the next is the captive. We are all captives by nature—led captive by the devil, by the world, by our own corrupt hearts; we are led captive by the devil at his will; by nature we tempt the devil to tempt us; we love the broad way; we hate God and his laws, and bid God depart from us; we are willing drudges to the devil. Again, we are to preach recovering of sight to the blind. We are all by nature blind; and this is our great misfortune, we do not know it—we think we see. There are some men who think they are mighty seeing men, but they do not see; they say they see, and yet they do not see original sin—they do not see the corruption of their hearts. These poor creatures are blind. We are blind by nature; we know not the way, by nature, of being reconciled to God, more than a man born blind knows how to describe the sun. Once more, Christ says, "The Lord hath sent me to set at liberty them that are bruised." We are described as poor, broken, blind, bruised creatures. What a poor helpless creature is man in his natural state. . . . Our whole head is sick, our whole heart is faint; from the crown of the head to the sole of the foot, we are full of wounds, bruises, and putrefying sores. In our flesh dwelleth no good thing. . . . you are so bruised that you cannot walk and come to God.[8]

So unspeakably dreadful was the state of the unconverted in the mind of the Puritan pastor that many of their discourses centered on bringing the unregenerate to a sense of the misery of their state. In what may be one of the first

---

8 Whitefield, pp. 9–14.

pieces of evangelicalistic literature, Joseph Alleine devoted an entire chapter to revealing the miseries of the unconverted. In his introduction to this theme, Alleine pondered the difficult task of penetrating a heart that was in bondage to sin. The evangelist wrote:

> Which way then shall I come at the miserable object that I have to deal with? Who shall make the heart of stone relent, or the lifeless carcase to feel and move? That God who is able of stones to raise up Children unto Abraham, that raises the dead, and melts the mountains, and strikes water out of the flint, that loves to work beyond the hopes and belief of man, that peoples His church with dry bones—He is able to do this. Therefore I bow my knee to the most high God, and as our Saviour prayed at the sepulchre of Lazarus, and the Shunnamite ran to the man of God for her dead child, so your mourning minister carries you in the arms of prayer to that God in whom your help is found.[9]

Then in verbose detail, Alleine proceeded to unveil the "misery which, I confess, no tongue can unfold, no heart can sufficiently comprehend."[10] Alleine then listed with corresponding explanations the following miseries:

> 1. The infinite God is engaged against you.
> [1] His face is against you . . . Psalm 34:16.
> [2] His heart is against you . . . Jer. 15:1, Zech. 11:8.
> [3] All His attributes are against you . . . Deut. 32:41–42.
> [4] The holiness of God is against you . . . Job 25:5.
> [5] The power of God is mounted like a mighty cannon against you. The glory of God's power is to be displayed

---

9 Joseph Alleine, *An Alarm to the Unconverted* (1671; rpt. Carlisle, Pa.: Banner of Truth, 1978), p. 81.
10 Alleine, p. 83.

in the amazing confusion and destruction of them that
obey not the gospel.
[6] Sinner, the power of God's anger is against you.
[7] The wisdom of God is set to ruin you . . . Psalm
7:11–13.
[8] The truth of God is sworn against you. If He is faithful and truth, you must perish if you go on. The whole
creation of God is against you. Satan has his full power
over you. The guilt of all your sins lies like a mountain
upon you. Your raging lusts miserably enslave you. The
furnace of eternal vengeance is heated ready for you.
The law discharges all its threats and curses at you. The
gospel itself binds the sentence of eternal damnation
upon you.[11]

Only one solution existed in the minds of the Puritan
preacher that could rend the hold that sin had upon
mankind—the gospel of the Bible. In fact, the belief in the
power of the gospel message was so strong that they even saw
that the evangel was the only means of preventing men from
deception. Even if God was not pleased to bring the hearer
to a saving knowledge of His Son, the gospel in its truth as it
related to man and his sin could still prevent man from being
seduced by error. Thomas Case, a student at Christ Church,
Oxford, delivered a sermon in which the young pastor declared that the whole Scripture was a module of saving truth.
After establishing that evangelical words are sound words
and all gospel truth is of a healing nature, Case made this observation:

It is a marvelous antidote against error and seduction—
gospel truths in their series and dependence are a chain
of gold to tie the truth and the soul close together.

---

[11]Alleine, pp. 83–89.

> People would not be so easily trepanned into heresy, if
> they were acquainted with the concatenation of gospel-
> doctrines within themselves. As, for instance, men
> would not certainly be so easily complimented to wor-
> ship that idol of free-will and the power of nature were
> they well principled in the doctrine of the fall [and] the
> design of God in permitting of it, held out in scripture
> in such large and legible characters that he who runs
> may read (Psalm 51:5; I Cor. 1:29–31; &c.); if they did
> with sobriety of spirit observe what the scripture pro-
> claims concerning the impotency of the lapsed and ru-
> ined creature, man's helpless condition in himself
> (Rom. 5:6; Eph. 2:1), of the absolute necessity of the
> quickening, helping, and stablishing influence of the
> Spirit of Christ, etc. When a chain of pearls is broken,
> a single jewel is easily lost: divine truths are mutually
> preservative in their social embraces and coherence.[12]

The clear teaching of Holy Writ, concerning man's total
depravity and his inability to effect any graces from himself
and the miserableness of his condition before the Holy
Creator, prompted Stephen Charnock to ask: "How is it con-
ceivable that God should hate the sin and cherish the sinner,
with all his filth, in His bosom? That He should eternally
detest the crime and eternally hold the sinner in His
arms?"[13]

The Puritan view of man and his sin and God and His
holiness would prohibit any of those great heralds of the
gospel from making such a statement as, "God loves you and
has a wonderful plan for your life." One of the great pearls of
the gospel truth, which, if violated, would alter the

---

[12] Thomas Case, "Sermon 1," in *Puritan Sermons 1659–1689*,V:23.

[13] Stephen Charnock, *Discourses Upon the Existence and Attributes of God*
(1853; rpt. Grand Rapids: Baker, 981), II:65.

effectiveness of the evangel, was the biblical doctrine of depraved man. In the Morning Exercises at Cripplegate, London, September 1651, William Greenhill presented one of several sermons on the subject of "commending ourselves to every man's conscience in the sight of God" (2 Cor. 4:2). His sermon was entitled, "What Must and Can Persons Do Towards Their Own Conversion." Reverend Greenhill's twelfth conclusion capsulized the Puritan understanding of man, his sin, and his inability. Greenhill pressed home:

> Con. XII. Man's quickening, believing, repenting, or turning, are not acts of man in part, and partly of God; but they are wholly of God and from God. "You hath he quickened" (Eph. 2:1). They were "dead," and could not quicken themselves; it was he, the Lord. So, "No man can come to me, except the Father draw him" (John 6:44). This drawing, or causing the soul to believe in Christ, is wholly the Father's work. And Ephraim saith, "Turn thou me, and I shall be turned" (Jer. 31:18). He could not turn himself: if the Lord had not done it, it would never have been done. Paul saith, "It is not in him that wills," &c., "but in God," etc. (Rom. 9:16). The will and deed are of him, not of man (Phil. 2:13). It is the Lord who is *Causa totius entis* ["the Cause of all being"].[14]

Modern evangelism of the Finney type may have its greatest variance from Puritan evangelism at this point of doctrine. Finney was a clear-headed and self-confessed Pelagian in his doctrine of man; that is why he instituted his new measures. Where the Puritans taught and preached total inability in fallen man, Finney assumed plenary ability.

---

[14] William Greenhill, "What Must and Can Persons Do Towards Their Own Conversion," in *Puritan Sermons 1659-1689*, I:42.

Finney denied that fallen man was totally unable to repent, believe or do anything spiritually good without grace, and affirmed instead that "all men have the plenary ability to turn to God at any time."[15]

Modern-day aberrations of Finneyism are rampant in evangelicalism. Finney, along with his modern cohorts, would agree that man is a rebel, but is perfectly free at any time to lay down his weapons of rebellion in surrender.[16] Accordingly, the message of the gospel is altered from that of the Puritan divines in pressing home the truth to the conscience to that of presenting vividly "to man's mind reason for making the surrender; that is, the Spirit's work is confined to moral persuasion."[17] Man is always free to reject the persuasion.

Because of Finney's view of man and his natural ability, one can understand, although not necessarily agree with, Finney's view of the role of the pastor. By confining the Spirit's work to persuasion, Finney advocated every means of increasing the force and vividness with which truth impinged upon the mind. Whether one chose to use the most frenzied excitement, the most harrowing emotionalism, or the most nervewracking commotion to increase the persuasive atmosphere, a preacher was encouraged to view all such means as proper in evangelism. Finney expressed avid support of this principle:

------

[15] Charles G. Finney, *Revival Lectures*, (Broadview, Il.: Cicero Bible Press, n.d.), pp. 217–21.

[16] Finney, pp. 409–31.

[17] J. I. Packer, "Puritan Evangelism," *The Banner of Truth*, 9 (n.d.), p. 5.

To expect to promote religion without excitements is
unphilosophical and absurd . . . until there is sufficient
religious principle in the world to put down irreligious
excitements, it is vain to try to promote religion, except by counteracting excitements. . . . There must be
excitement sufficient to wake up the dormant moral
powers.[18]

Finney held that at any time, man could within himself
rouse up his dormant moral powers, lay down the gauntlet of
rebellion against God, and decide for Christ. Thus, as the
advocates of modern Finneyism demonstrate, the Puritan
role of the pastor as one called to preach a message of truth
that is pressed home to the conscience and is alone the
power of God unto salvation, has been exchanged for one
which has as its principal duty preaching for immediate
decision. Using means such as the rousing appeal and the
altar call are seen as consistent with the role of the pastor to
persuade the sinner to decide for Christ.

Finney and his modern counterparts view evangelistic
preaching as a battle of wills between the preacher and the
hearer. Such a view leads to the assumption that it is the responsibility of the preacher to bring the hearers to the
breaking point by persuading them to "present and instant
acceptance of His will, present and instant acceptance of
Christ."[19]

One's view of man and his ability affects one's view of
his responsibility in preaching. To the Puritans, who held
that man was totally depraved, salvation was seen as a work
of Divine grace, Divine power, and Divine sovereignty. To

---

[18] Finney, p. 212.

[19] Charles G. Finney, *Autobiography* (Broadview, Il.: Cicero Bible Press,
n.d.), p. 64.

Finney and many of his modern followers, methodology became the byword in preaching. With such a Pelagian view of man as held by Finney, methodology must of necessity express itself if preaching is to become aggressively evangelistic.

Finney is remembered for his methods; the Puritans are remembered for their message.

Chapter 4

The View of the Person and Work of Christ

Puritan preaching was not the offer of the possibility of salvation, but the offer of the Savior Himself. They preached a salvation that was full and perfect. Their message was an evangel of the all-sufficiency and suitability of the person of Christ as the sole substitute for the sinner. They preached a message about who Christ was, what He had done, and what He was able to do. To preach Christ meant to present the person of Christ as well as His finished work of satisfaction. While serving as the Dean of Christ Church and the Vice-Chancellor of the University of Oxford, John Owen wrote in a rebuttal against Popery:

> It is a general notion of truth, that the Lord Jesus Christ, in his person and grace, is to be proposed and presented unto men as the principal object of their faith and love.[1]

In making specific mention of the contents of biblical preaching, Owen stated that the power that is in the Word of God consists in its efficacy to communicate the grace of God unto the souls of men.

---

[1] John Owen, "An Antidote against Popery," in *Puritan Sermons 1659-1689*, translator James Nichols (rpt. Wheaton: Richard Owen Roberts, 1981), III:215.

The grace of God was seen in the person and the work of Christ as contained in the gospel. Owen said:

> There must therefore an image or representation of him be made unto our minds, or he cannot be the proper object of our faith, trust, love, and delight. This is done in the gospel, and the preaching of it; for therein he is "evidently set forth before our eyes as crucified amongst us" (Gal. 3:1). So also are all the other concerns of his person and offices therein clearly proposed unto us: yea, this is the principal end of the gospel, namely, to make a due representation of the person, offices, grace, and glory of Christ, unto the souls of men, that they may believe in him, and, believing, have eternal life (John 10:31).[2]

The all-sufficiency of His person and work was a major theme in dealing with the heresies of Romanism. Thomas Lye preached a sermon in the Cripplegate Exercises that dealt with works of supererogation; his defense was "the all-fullness of satisfaction that made ample amends to God's enraged justice."

The combination of the person and the work was revealed by Lye:

> The fulness of Christ's satisfaction is . . . plain from the infinite worthiness of his person. . . . The great acceptableness of this sacrifice unto God proceeds from the dignity of the priest offering—the eternal Son of God, in whom God was infinitely well pleased. . . . Tell me, then, is there in Christ's humiliation an all-fulness of satisfaction to divine justice, yea, or no? If so, what need then is the least of this fig-leaf of human satisfaction? To what purpose do we light up a dim taper and a

---

2 Owen, pp. 215–216.

smokey candle, when we have before us the clear and full light of a mid-day sun? If Christ's satisfaction be of infinite price, why may it not serve for the expiation of the guilt of temporal, as well as eternal, punishment? If there be an all-sufficiency in Christ's satisfaction, what need the supplement of ours?[3]

To these great expositors of biblical truth, the sufficiency of His saviorhood rested upon the salvation He accomplished once for all when He satisfied God's law upon the cross and rose again in triumphant power and glory. The resurrection guaranteed the continued activity at the right hand of the Father. The unchangeable priesthood of Christ made His continued work efficacious and complete. Christ's continuing work in the heavenlies in His priestly role was seen as the reason why He was able to save those who came unto Him and to give them eternal life. When the Puritans presented Christ to lost men in the heralding of the gospel, He was represented as a Savior who ever continued to be the embodiment of the salvific work that He had once for all accomplished. Thus, the Puritan divines offered not a possibility of salvation, but the person who accomplished salvation, full and complete.

Many of the Puritans considered preaching Christ a difficult task. The difficulty was not in the motive or the subject matter; the difficulty was to adequately convey truth to deaf ears, and not succumb to the temptation of preaching for admiration. Thomas Brooks penned these words of admonition to a gathering of fellow pastors:

---

3 Thomas Lye, "There Are Not Any Works of Supererogation," in *Puritan Sermons 1659-1689*, VI:244.

> First, Jesus Christ must be preached plainly, perspicu-
> ously, so as the meanest capacity may understand what
> they say concerning Christ. They must preach Christ
> for edification, and not for admiration, as too many do in
> these days. . . . He is not the best preacher that tickles
> the ear, or that works upon the fancy, &c., but he that
> breaks the heart and awakens the conscience.[4]

The great phobia of these men was the fear of appealing to
the senses and the emotions rather than to the conscience of
the hearer. Consequently, Christ and His work were presented in terms of completion or perfection to impress upon
the darkened conscience the grace of God in dealing with the
heinousness of man's depraved state. The tenderhearted
John Flavel wrote:

> The effect and fruit of this his satisfaction, is our free-
> dom, ransom, or deliverance from the wrath and curse
> due to us for our sins. Such was the dignity, value, and
> completeness of Christ's satisfaction, that in strict jus-
> tice it merited our redemption and full deliverance; not
> only a possibility that we might be redeemed and par-
> doned, but a right whereby to be so.[5]

Of course, this emphasis upon the person and work of
Christ, and not the emphasis on the possibility of salvation in
Christ, had its roots in their view of man and his total inability to choose Christ apart from the intervention of God's
grace. Flavel stated:

---

[4] Thomas Brooks, *The Complete Works of Thomas Brooks* (1861; rpt.
Carlisle, Pa.: Banner of Truth, 1980), III:211–12.
[5] John Flavel, *The Works of John Flavel* (Carlisle, Pa.: Banner of Truth,
1982), I:181.

> The priesthood of Christ presupposeth the utter im-
> potency of men to appease God, and recover by any
> thing he could do or suffer. Surely God would not come
> down to assume a body to die, and be offered up for us if
> at any cheaper rate it could have been accomplished;
> there was no other way to recover man and satisfy God.[6]

As these preachers focused on the work of the Savior,
eloquent descriptions of His person poured forth from their
lips and pens. One constantly reads of such descriptions as
"the excellencies of Jesus Christ," or "the loveliest person
souls can set their eyes upon" as human attempts to verbally
ascribe to Him His value and worth.[7] In a sermon entitled,
"Yea, He Is Altogether Lovely," Flavel presented a myriad
of reasons why it "is said of Jesus Christ, which cannot be
said of any other creature; that he is altogether lovely." His
propositions included:

> First, He is altogether lovely in his person: a Diety
> dwelling in flesh, John 1:14. . . . Secondly, He is alto-
> gether lovely in his offices; The suitableness of the of-
> fices of Christ to the miseries and wants of men; the
> fulness of his offices become an universal relief to all
> our wants; unspeakably comfortable must the offices of
> Christ be to the souls of sinners. . . . Thirdly, Jesus
> Christ is altogether lovely in his relations . . . He is a
> lovely Redeemer . . . He is a lovely bridegroom. . . .
> Fourthly, Christ is altogether lovely, in the relation of
> an Advocate. . . . Fifthly, Christ is altogether lovely in
> the relation of a friend. . . . [8]

Then in the classic Puritan tradition of listing a series of

---

6 Flavel, I:245.
7 Flavel, II:215.
8 Flavel, II:215–224.

uses in the application of a stated doctrine, Flavel beseeched his hearers "to set your souls upon this lovely Jesus. Methinks such an object as hath been presented, should compel love from the coldest breast and hardest heart."[9]

As part of the questions addressed at the Morning Exercises at Cripplegate, Robert Traill preached a sermon in response to the question, "By what means may ministers best win souls?" In his address by the same name, Traill revealed the mindset of Puritan preaching as it related to the work of Christ. Pastor Traill instructed:

> About the end, the winning of souls. This is to bring them to God. It is not to win them to us, or to engage them into a party, or to the espousal of some opinions and practices, supposing them to be never so right, and consonant to the word of God. But the winning of them is, to bring them out of nature into a state of grace, that they may be fitted for, and in due time admitted into everlasting glory.[10]

The imagery of winning people to Christ consisted of translating people into the presence of God by faith, and not that of bringing God down to meet the whimsical needs of man. After all, the Puritans believed that man did not even know his needs; therefore, how could an unregenerate person be expected to correctly ask God to do anything other than fulfill his selfish desires? Such application of the gospel was a belittlement of the glories of Christ and His finished work. Concerning the subject matter of gospel preaching,

---

[9] Flavel, II:224.

[10] Robert Traill, *The Works of Robert Traill*, Vol. I (1810; rpt. Carlisle, Pa.: Banner of Truth, 1975), I:243–244.

Traill continued:

> To things ministers have to do about him in preaching
> him to them that are without. 1. To set him forth to
> people, Gal. 3:1; to paint him in his love, excellency,
> and ability to save. 2. To offer him unto them freely,
> fully, without any limitation as to sinners, or their sinful
> state. . . . How little of Jesus Christ is there in some
> pulpits! It is seen as to success, that whatever the law
> doth in alarming sinners, it is still the gospel-voice that
> is the key that opens the heart to Jesus Christ. Would
> ministers win souls? Let them have more of Jesus
> Christ in their dealing with men, and less of benefits to
> man that he thinks are his that never profit them that
> are exercised therein.[11]

The concern that guided the Puritans in their preaching
was an awareness that, if they appealed only to the emotions,
souls could be deceived into mere belief because of the at-
tractiveness of what Christ had to offer. Using as his text
Luke 7:31–35, Richard Sibbes spoke on the subject of "The
Success of the Gospel." After great deliberation in ascribing
to man the inability to choose, Sibbes concluded:

> Observe, that where grace doth not overpower nature,
> no means will prevail over the obdurate nature of man.
> Neither John nor Christ would work anything upon
> these Pharisees. Thus was it in the wilderness and
> Egypt. What admirable wonders did God work, yet how
> incredulous and stiffnecked were they! And the reason
> is, God gave not a heart, and in the conversion of a sin-
> ner there must be another manner of grace than only
> offering and exhortation to accept of Christ; nay, the
> Spirit itself must do more than exhort, for it may lay

---

[11] Traill, I:243–246.

open to us many motives, tell us of God's goodness, truth, and strength sealed to us; it may tell us of wrath and judgment, and on the other side of kingdoms, everlasting joys, perfection of happiness, yet all not work any remorse in the heart of man if the Spirit leaves him there. And the reason is, man is dead in sin by nature, and that "strong man" having gotten the possession, cannot be cast out by the "stronger man," which must quicken and give power, that may change every part of the soul, the understanding, will, and affections, else all means is to no purpose but for to make us inexcusable at the day of judgment. Hence therefore we may see the shallowness of those that conceive of the word of God, as if it did only persuade the will to choose. No; it must alter the will and change it quite, else benefits are to no purpose.[12]

Puritan preaching focused on the person and work of Jesus Christ; and the offer of the gospel was to trust Him and a salvation that was full and perfect. They did not offer the possibility of salvation and its benefits; they offered the Person who accomplished the benefits. This is not the case with much of modern evangelism and preaching. Laws Two, Three, and Four of "The Four Spiritual Laws," published by Campus Crusade for Christ, contain the phrase, "know and experience God's love and plan for his (your, our) life (lives)." While Jesus Christ is presented as "God's only provision for man's sin" (Law Three), the emphasis is on what man receives, that is, experiencing God's love and plan for one's life, and not who Christ was, what He accomplished, and what He is able to do.

Our fear should be the same as that of our Puritan

---

[12] Richard Sibbes, *The Works of Richard Sibbes*, ed. Alexander B. Grosart (rpt. Carlisle: Banner of Truth, 1973-81), VII:281f.

brethren—sinners will be drawn to what Jesus will do or give them rather than to understanding what Christ has accomplished for them. The danger, as forewarned by the evangelists of an earlier century, is that man will give his mental assent to the promises claimed and not have his heart altered by the Person proclaimed. In many cases, the latter is not possible today because the person of Christ is only presented in reference to the benefits associated with receiving Christ.

During the summer of 1984 in Los Angeles, a major evangelical thrust was organized to reach the thousands of people either attending or competing in the Olympic Games. A massive literature distribution campaign was one of the mechanisms designed to proclaim the gospel. Granted, such tracts do not fill the position of preaching; nevertheless, the content of the literature is indicative of the messages that fill the churches of our land. One such piece distributed by Jews for Jesus was entitled, "I Thought I Was an Olympic Superstar." The tract pictured the person and work of Christ thusly:

> I thought I was an Olympic superstar! I couldn't throw a javelin, but I could do very well at running the rat race . . . hurling the insult . . . jumping on the bandwagon, wrestling with anxiety.
>
> I took comfort from knowing that I could participate every day (not just once every four years)! I constructed my own game plan.
>
> In my olympics, there were no judges. I was the sole contestant, and I played the game my way. But I never made it into the *Guinness Book of World Records*. In my events, there were no winners. And I started to wonder why I was running so furiously if I never won.
>
> Then, I made a discovery. I found out that there was a judge after all. He wasn't Zeus thundering from Mount

Olympus. He was the God of the universe, living in the
Poconos and everywhere else!

And God's ruling against me was: "Gong—
Disqualified!" That's when I realized that there was a
better game to play and a better race to run.

Saul, also known as Paul, said it like this: "Forgetting
what is behind and straining toward what is ahead, I
press on toward the goal to win the prize for which God
has called me heavenward in the Messiah, Y'shua"
(Phil. 3:13–14).

Running on God's track and playing by His rules is
much more satisfying than any earthly event. Follow
God's game plan. Let Him call the shots and qualify you
for a Crown of Life. Want to make it into Y'shua's Book
of Life? Write or call.[13]

The same organization published another tract parodying
Michael Jackson musical hits entitled, "Can You Find 36
Michael Jackson Song Titles in This Pamphlet?" The pam-
phlet featured sketches of the musician dancing and singing
and concluded with the following statement concerning
Christ:

It is in the strength of one man that we can change the
world. It's really as simple as ABC. The man God sent
was Y'shua (Jesus); and if you believe with a child's heart
that Y'shua is Lord and confess that God raised Him
from the dead, you will be saved. Don't tell God to beat
it or say, maybe tomorrow, because God is saying, "I
want you back now." Give God one more chance.[14]

Modern evangelical preaching places at its center the offer and reception of eternal life. Such statements as, "Have

---

[13] Jews for Jesus pamphlet #BR 257 (1984).
[14] Jews for Jesus pamphlet #BR 259 (1984).

you come to the place in your spiritual life where you can know for certain that if you were to die today you would go to heaven?"[15] are used to direct the sinner's attention to the instructions that follow concerning Christ. The crux of Puritan preaching was reconciliation to God from which eternal life was a result, but not the object of the proclamation. Reconciliation was tied to the horridness of sin and could only be achieved by the death of Christ. The Scottish Divine Thomas Boston said of this relationship:

> Here we may see the horrid and hateful evil of sin, which no other sacrifice could expiate but the blood of the Son of God. As the strength of a disease is known and seen by the quality and force of the medicine that is made use of to cure it, and the virtue of a commodity by the greatness of the price that is laid down to buy it, so is the matter here. The sufferings and death of Christ express the evil of sin far above the severest judgments that ever were inflicted upon any creature.[16]

In the Puritan mind, the work of reconciliation was the work of the gospel. John Flavel remarked:

> The work whereunto the ministers of the gospel are appointed, is to reconcile the world to God; to work these sinful, vain, rebellious hearts, which have a strong aversion from God naturally in them, to close with him according to the articles of peace contained in the gospel, that thereby they may be capable to receive the mercies and benefits purchased by the death of Christ,

---

[15] D. James Kennedy, *Evangelism Explosion* (1970, Wheaton: Tyndale, 1973), pp. 30–31.

[16] Thomas Boston, *The Beauties of Boston* (1831; rpt. Inverness, Scotland: Christian Focus Publications, 1979), p. 206.

which they cannot receive in the state of enmity and alienation.[17]

Benefits to man, such as eternal life, were seen as the result of reconciliation. Again, from the pen of John Flavel:

> Now reconciliation with God, is the restoring of men to that former friendship they had with God, which was broken by the fall, and is still continued by our enmity and aversion whilst we continue in our natural and unregenerate state. Now this is the greatest and most blessed design that ever God had in the world; and astonishing and invaluable mercy to men.[18]

In summation, the great Puritan mentor concluded that "this reconciliation with God is the fountain out of which all other comforts flow to us."

In a system which presupposes that man is capable of responding to a reasonable presentation of benefits that will be accrued to his account, man naturally becomes the reason for the work of Christ. Such is modern Finneyism. But to the Puritans, God was the reason for the work of Christ, because God alone could accomplish and apply the finished work of Christ to the sinner.

---

[17] Flavel, II:50.
[18] Flavel, I:477.

Chapter 5

The View of Repentance and Faith

The Puritans taught, as a general rule, that conviction of sin produced by the preaching of the law would precede faith, since no man was capable of coming to Christ to be saved in his or her own strength. This conviction in the heart and the mind of a sinner became known in Puritan theology as "preparation for faith" or "preparation for salvation."[1] It was also known in New England circles, propagated mainly by Solomon Stoddard and his grandson Jonathan Edwards, as "seeking salvation." This concept became one of the distinctive features of the Puritan doctrine of conversion. The process can be summarized by the following: convincing, conviction, contrition, and conversion. J. I. Packer described the conversion doctrine of the Puritans:

> Man's first step toward conversion must be some knowledge of God, of himself, of his duty, and his sin. The second step is conviction, both of sinfulness and of particular sins; and the wise minister, dealing with the enquirers at this stage, would try to deepen conviction and make it specific, since true and sound conviction of sin is always to a greater or lesser degree particularised. This led to contrition (sorrow for and hatred of sin), which began to turn the love of sinning out of the heart and led to real, though as yet ineffective, attempts to break off the practice of sin in the life. A Puritan minister, seeing that the above process had been begun in

---

[1] J. I. Packer, "Puritan Evangelism," *The Banner of Truth* (n.d.), p. 10.

the heart of the sinner, would then urge the hearer to come to Christ. Puritan pastors believed that was the right advice to give to a person who had shown with his heart that he desired to be saved from sin. Only when a man wanted to be saved from sin was it possible for him "genuinely and sincerely to receive the One who presents Himself to man as the Saviour from sin."[2]

The Puritans understood that salvation was not possible otherwise; therefore they urged ministers never to short-circuit the essential preparatory process. They sought never to give false encouragement to those in whom this preparation had not done its work. Throughout the whole ministry of preparation, from the first glimpses of awakening to the ultimate dawning of faith, the sovereignty of God was recognized as supreme. Thomas Brooks stated that:

> None can freely, seriously, habitually, resolutely, choose God and Christ, grace and glory, holiness and happiness, as their *summun bonum*, chiefest good, but such who are really good . . . as our love to God is but an effect of his love to us . . . so our choosing of God for our God is but an effect of God's choosing us for his people.[3]

Thus, in the words of Richard Baxter, God was viewed as the cause of such conviction:

> God, as the most laudable, principal cause, doth cause man's will to turn itself. The instrumental cause is the doctrine of Christ, either read, or heard, or some way known, and brought by the Spirit to men's understanding and consideration.

---

[2] *Ibid*, p. 10.

[3] Thomas Brooks, *The Complete Works of Thomas Brooks* (1861; rpt. Carlisle, Pa.: Banner of Truth, 1980), III:382.

The need of such conviction was based upon their view of the heinous condition of man before God. They saw that "God finds nothing in man to excite His love, but much to provoke His loathing."[4]

In one's unconverted state, the sinner was not only without God, but also God was against the sinner. Thus, a sinner under conviction had to deal with two issues: God and His Mediator. Repentance and faith were the two graces God supplied through His act of regeneration, of renewing the heart and mind, to deal with one's conviction; thus, the renewed heart and mind had to act according to its nature. The application of repentance and faith were, to the Puritans, the responsibility of man, whereas regeneration was the act of God. In a sermon on Acts 2:37–38, Thomas Manton touched on the duality of repentance and faith as necessary for salvation:

> The Lord himself must state the terms upon which his grace shall be dispensed; now he hath appointed the way: Acts 3:19, "Repent ye, therefore, and be converted, that your sins may be blotted out when the times of refreshment shall come from the presence of the Lord." Repentance is a means or condition, or moral qualification on our parts: it is *conditio sine qua non*, without which we are not capable of the benefit. The first moving cause is the mercy and grace of God: Isa. xliii. 25, "I, even I am he that blotteth out thy transgressions for mine own sake, and will not remember thy sin." The meritorious and procuring cause is the blood of Christ: Eph. i. 7, 'In whom we have redemption through his blood, the forgiveness of sin.' That is the satisfaction given to God for our

---

[4] Richard Baxter, *The Practical Works of Richard Baxter* (Ligonier, Pa.: Soli Deo Gloria, 1990), II:64.

offences, to repair him in point of honour. But the
causes do not exclude our duty; there must be something
done on our part by way of application to make our right
and title clear, and that is faith and repentance: these
two sister graces, the one respects God and the other
the Mediator Jesus Christ: "Repentance towards God,
and faith in our Lord Jesus Christ," Acts xx. 21. The
offence is done to God, and he is the party to whom we
return by Christ. These two graces go hand in hand, and
we must not put asunder what God hath joined
together.[5]

The Puritan saw these two graces working together in a
logical sequence as well as from a Divine mandate. Faith was
directed to salvation from sin; therefore, there must be a ha-
tred of sin and a desire to be saved from sin. One of the most
grievous wrongs a minister could do to a person being drawn
to God by the work of the Spirit in regeneration was to tell
the sinner to stop worrying about his sins and trust Christ at
once if he did not yet know his sins and did not yet have a
desire to forsake them.[6] The Puritans understood repentance
to be turning from sin unto God and by necessity that
turning to God implied faith in the mercy of God as revealed
in the Mediator Jesus Christ.[7] A Puritan could not, therefore, separate repentance and faith. While they worked
together, they did not argue as to which grace occurred first.
Manton noted: "If you ask which goes first? that is hard to
say: there is not such a distinction of time in the work of
conversion that we can tell which is first or which is last:

---

[5] Thomas Manton, *The Complete Works of Thomas Manton* (rpt.
Worthington, Pa.: Maranatha Publications, n.d.), XXI:265.

[6] Packer, p. 10.

[7] Manton, XXI:263–265.

the work is intermingled."[8]

Ezekiel Hopkins analyzed this interdependence by comparing it to the progression of sin: "As one sin doth draw upon another, by conscience likewise doth one grace draw upon another."[9] These ministers of the doctrines of grace observed that the faith which was unto salvation was a faith which was accompanied by a change of thought and attitude. Repentance consisting of a change of heart, mind, and will affected one's attitude toward four things: God, oneself, sin, and righteousness.[10] As previously discussed, the Puritans knew that apart from regeneration one's thought patterns were radically perverted. Regeneration radically renewed a sinner's mind; hence there was a radical change in one's thinking and feeling. Regeneration became vocal in the mind of the sinner in the exercises of repentance and faith.

At the same time, the Puritans did not think that repentance consisted merely of a general change of mind. They perceived it to be very particular and concrete. Christopher Love warned against misreading one's feelings by admonishing sinners:

> Be sure you do not mistake moral persuasion to be the Spirit's working in you. Moral persuasions do not reach but to the outward man, but the Spirit's operations to the inward man. Moral persuasions only restrain the acts of sin, but the Spirit's working debilitates the habits of sin. Moral persuasions only make a man forbear sin

---

[8] Manton, XXI:265.

[9] Ezekiel Hopkins, *The Works of Ezekiel Hopkins* (London: Jonathan Robinson, 1701), p. 814 (This title, in a later 3 volume edition, has been reprinted by Soli Deo Gloria).

[10] Thomas Boston, *The Complete Works of Thomas Boston* (rpt. Wheaton: Richard Owen Roberts, 1980), VI:397.

> rather for fear of punishment than out of love to holi-
> ness, or hatred of sin with respect to God.[11]

Since repentance was a change of mind with reference to sin, there had to be a change of mind with reference to particular, individual sins. After all, how could an individual change their mind about sin if he did not know his sins? John Bradford remarked concerning individual awareness of sins: "As when a man is sick, the first step to health is to know his sickness; even so to salvation, the first step is to know thy damnation due for thy sins."[12]

With the stress on the importance of repentance and faith, the Puritans at the same time maintained that neither one of these duties had any meritorious value to them. David Clarkson reminded his audience:

> Think not that your repentance can satisfy God, or
> make any amends for the wrong sin has done Him; do
> not imagine that it is any recompense for the injury sin
> has done Him, or any reparation of that honor which is
> violated and defaced by sin. . . . It is a mercy that our
> repentance is not yet punished, much more that it is
> rewarded.[13]

Repentance to the Puritans described the response of turning from sin unto God; faith described the response of receiving and resting upon Christ alone for salvation.

---

[11] Christopher Love, *The Combat Between the Flesh and the Spirit* (London: Thomas Cole, 1656), p. 76. This work has been reprinted by Soli Deo Gloria as Volume 1 of *The Works of Christopher Love*.

[12] John Bradford, *The Works of John Bradford* (1853; rpt. Carlisle, Pa.: Banner of Truth, 1979), I:43.

[13] David Clarkson, *The Works of David Clarkson* (1864, James Nichols, Edinburgh) I:20.

Thomas Adams correctly summarized the mindset of his fellow Puritans by stating that "if we believe not we are yet in our sins; if we repent not, our sins are still in us."[14] As Ezekiel Hopkins penned, "It is impossible for men by their own strength and natural ability to become Christians, but it is possible for God to make them Christians."[15] The Puritans believed that God did not pierce each person's heart in the same manner or in the same time frame. Describing this varied work, J. I. Packer concluded:

> God converts no adult without preparing him; but "God breaketh not all men's hearts alike" (Baxter). Some conversions, as Goodwin said, are sudden; the preparation is done in a moment. Some are long-drawn-out affairs; years may pass before the seeker finds Christ and peace, as in Bunyan's case. . . . No rule can be given as to how long, or how intensely, God will flay each sinner with the lash of conviction. Thus the work of effectual calling proceeds as fast, or as slow, as God wills. The Puritan minister viewed his part in the process of conversion as that of a midwife, whose task was to see what was happening and give appropriate help at each stage. They also realized they could not foretell, let alone fix, how rapid the process of birth would be. Since God convinced, convicted, and converted a sinner through His Word, the Puritan preacher saw as his task in evangelism the declaration of God's mind as revealed in the passage they expounded, the showing of the lost the way to salvation, and the exhortation of the unbelievers to learn the law, to meditate on God's Word, and to humble themselves before God by praying that God would show them their sins and give them the grace necessary

---

[14] Thomas Adams, *The Works of Thomas Adams* (1630; rpt. Edinburgh: James Nichols, 1862), III:126.
[15] Hopkins, p. 818.

to enable them to come to Christ.[16]

Such a mindset can be observed in a prayer by Bradford:

> Merciful Father of our Saviour Jesus Christ, because I
> have sinned and done wickedly, and through thy good-
> ness I have received a desire of repentance, whereto this
> longsuffering doth draw my hard heart, I beseech thy
> mercy in Christ to work the same repentance in me;
> and by thy Spirit, power and grace, to humble, mortify,
> and sear my conscience for my sins to salvation, that in
> thy time thou mayest quicken me again through Jesus
> Christ, thy dearly loved Son. Amen.[17]

The Puritan expositors would charge their audiences to
hold forth Christ as a perfect Savior from sin, and would
invite the weary and burdened souls to come to the Savior
who waited to receive them. They did not invite the hearers
to do something with Christ, but they exhorted the audience
to plead with God to do something with them. While
Charles Finney preached a message of repentance and faith,
the Puritans would never do what Finney stressed should be
done in demanding immediate repentance and faith of all
persons. The Puritans believed that repentance and faith
were graces that God produced in the regenerated heart; to
Finney, they were something to do. In his lectures on revival preaching, Finney stated:

> Sinners ought to be made to feel that they have some-
> thing to do, and that is, to repent; that it is something
> which no other being can do for them, neither God nor
> man; and something to do, not something to wait for.

---

[16] Packer, p. 10.
[17] Bradford, I:43.

> And they must do it now, or they are in danger of eternal death.[18]

While the Puritans would agree that man must fulfill the duty of repenting, and that it was their preaching responsibility to tell all men that they must repent and believe to be saved, they would not go further and tell all the unconverted that they ought to "decide for Christ" on the spot. Only those who had been drawn by the Spirit and were prepared could believe; it was only those whom God summoned to believe; anyone else doing so, or attempting to do so, would be doing a self-imposed work. Finney supposed that the unconverted had the power to accept Christ at any moment even though he recognized there were different degrees of being awakened.[19] Much of modern evangelism has gone beyond Finney by either adulterating the message of repentance or by totally eliminating it from the content of the gospel. An example of the latter would be the following statement taken from a handbook on evangelism used at the Florida Bible College: "Any teaching that demands a change of conduct toward either God or man for salvation is to add works or human effort to faith, and this contradicts all Scripture and is an accursed message."[20]

As a result of either a weakened or an eliminated position on repentance, modern Finneyism assumes it is the evangelist's prerogative to fix the time when men shall first savingly believe.[21] To do so, in the eyes of the Puritans, would be an

---

[18] Charles G. Finney, *Revival Lectures* (Broadview, Il.: Cicero Bible Press, n.d.), p. 232.

[19] Finney, pp. 180–192.

[20] A. Ray Stanford, *Handbook of Personal Evangelism* (Florida Bible College, n.d.), p. 37.

[21] Finney, pp. 180–192.

act of presumption, however creditable the minister's motive may be. For a pastor to fix the time by appealing to sinners to begin believing immediately would be, to the great Puritan divines, taking upon themselves the sovereign right of God the Holy Spirit. The appeal for an immediate decision without proper preparation by the Spirit of God presupposes that men are free to accept Christ as their Savior at any time. The Puritans' view of sin prevented such a presupposition. Concerning repentance, Samuel Cradock stated, "'Tis not the falling into sin which is man's final ruin, but the continuing in it, and not recovering a man's self out of it again, by repentance, and recourse to Christ's blood."[22] Concerning faith, John Bradford stated: "Faith is so far from the reach of man's freewill, that to reason it is plain foolishness."[23]

Such were the Puritan views of repentance and faith; only God could produce them, but man was responsible for them.

---

[22] Samuel Cradock, *Knowledge and Practice* (London: William Grantham 1673), p. 217.
[23] Bradford. I:43.

Chapter 6

The View of Assurance

Of all the doctrines preached by the Puritans, their instructions concerning the assurance of salvation may have prompted the greatest joy as well as the greatest misunderstanding. Modern theologians have judged the Puritans to teach a salvation by works because of the strong emphasis they placed on visible evidence of saving faith. While recognizing that assurance was not essential (they made the distinction between the *esse* and the *bene esse* of something) to one's salvation, the Puritans did instruct their flocks to "remember that the process of faith to assurance is gradual. As it arises from a knowledge of Jesus, be diligent in searching the Scriptures, which testify of Him."[1] Because of their view of God and of man's depravity, the Puritans truly believed in hell and recognized their awful responsibility should they give some persons cause to believe they were saved without evidence.

As convinced as they were of the need of visible evidence in the believer's life, the Puritan preachers also were comforting in their exhortations to the faint-hearted. They understood that faith, being a gift of God, had different degrees of expression. Thomas Brooks remarked:

> He that cannot find in himself the evidences of a strong
> faith, he must not conclude that he has no faith; for he

---

1 John Newton, *The Works of John Newton* (New York: Robert Carter and Brothers, 1856), p. 481.

> may have in him the evidences of a weak faith when he
> has not the evidences of a strong faith in him.[2]

Continuing to reveal the compassionate heart of a pastor
for his fledglings, Brooks affirmed:

> In Christ's school, house, church, there are several sorts
> and ranks of Christians, as babes, children, young men,
> and old men; and accordingly ministers, in their
> preaching and writing, should sort their evidences so
> that babes and children may not be found bleeding,
> grieving, and weeping, when they should be found joy-
> ing and rejoicing.[3]

"Every real Christian hath in some measure every sancti-
fying grace in him"[4] was the mindset that dictated the
Puritan approach to instructing believers to seek some evidence of saving graces before experiencing the calm of assurance. Therefore, sermons dealing with hindrances to assurance, difficulties to assurance, and steps to gaining assurance
are myriad in the period literature.

Quite often, faith and assurance were attested to as being
identical. John Newton, writing on this union, stated:

> The grounds and principles of faith and assurance are
> exactly the same. The first and lowest act of saving faith
> necessarily includes these things: (A) An apprehension
> of the sufficiency and authority of Christ to save; (B)
> An application of Him; (C) A hope in His mercy,
> which is fainter or stronger according as the knowledge

---

[2] Thomas Brooks, *The Works of Thomas Brooks* (1861; rpt. Carlisle, Pa.:
Banner of Truth, 1980), III:252.
[3] *Ibid.*
[4] Brooks, III:255.

of Jesus is more or less distinct.[5]

The basis for such assurance was the Word of God. Warning his flock against seeking assurance from other means than the Word, Thomas Brooks heralded:

> There is, especially in times of great afflictions, temptations, desertions, fears, and doubts, a very great aptness and proneness in Christians to expect strange means rather than right means, and new means rather than old means, and invented means rather than appointed means, and to build their faith upon something other than the word.[6]

After lengthy exhortations to use the Scripture to judge all disputes concerning one's salvation, Brooks concluded, "Til a man comes to be willing to have his spiritual and eternal estate to be determined by Scripture, he will never enjoy any settled rest or quiet in his spirit."[7]

The use of the Scripture as the final issue in determining one's confirmation of assurance prevented the Puritan preachers from giving false hope to the unregenerate, and placed them in the position of directing the falsely convinced to the feet of the Savior. At the same time, they stressed the joyous hope of being assured that one was in a state of grace. This hope was not a mere conjectural or probable persuasion, but an infallible assurance of faith based upon the divine promises of salvation, the inward graces of the Holy Spirit, and the outward testimony of altered con-

---

[5] Newton, p. 481.
[6] Brooks, III:263.
[7] Brooks, III:264.

duct in response to sin.[8]

For the Puritans, assurance was solely a ministry of the
Holy Spirit and could not be performed by or given by men.
Even though one might encounter diverse conflicts and
difficulties in gaining assurance, every true believer could
be enabled by the Spirit to know the things that were freely
given by God. Therefore, they viewed it as the personal
responsibility of every believer to give all diligence to make
one's calling and election sure in order to experience the joy
and peace and cheerfulness in duties of obedience required
by one's Master.[9]

Perhaps it is at this point that many misinterpret the
Puritan emphasis. They were not preaching a works-
oriented faith; rather, they were instructing the converted to
use the right means to confirm in their hearts, by the ministry of the Spirit, the joys of seeing the fruits of assurance.
Their perspective was "if thou keep not the precept, thou
hast no part in the promise."[10] Oftentimes gaining assurance
was a struggle. Thomas Adams acknowledged:

> The devil labors to secure men of God's providence
> generally, though they be quite out of the way. He bids
> men be confident that God will keep their souls, howso-
> ever they walk. So under the colour of God's protection,
> he brings them to destruction. He tells a man of pre-
> destination, that he is sure of eternal election to life,
> therefore may live at his own pleasure, and so from
> God's decrees draws encouragements to a secure life. He

[8] Thomas Doolittle, "Assurance Is Possible," in *Puritan Sermons 1659–
1689*, editor James Nichols (rpt. Wheaton: Richard Owen Roberts,
1981), I:252–283.
[9] Doolittle, I:252–83.
[10] Thomas Adams, *The Works of Thomas Adams* (1630; rpt. Edinburgh:
James Nichols, 1862), III:137.

tells him of justification, that he is acquitted by the blood of Christ, so emboldens him on the back of presumption to ride post to hell, whereas predestination and justification are only made known to us by "welldoing."[11]

Acquiring heavenly assurance was not only a responsibility, but also a deterrent from sin. John Tillotson wrote: "Had we the same awe and regard for the threatenings and promises of the Gospel that we have for the smiles and frowns of those who are in power and authority, even this would be effectual to keep us from sin."[12]

The combination of the ministry of the Spirit of God providing inward confidence and outward evidence formulated the Puritan doctrine of assurance. To these shepherds of God's flock, the difference between biblical and counterfeit assurance would "only be gained in holy and heavenly ways, and always according to the Word."[13]

Very clear instructions were given to souls in order to assist them in confirming God's work of grace in one's life. In a work appropriately titled, "Heaven On Earth," Thomas Brooks provided the following list: "There are seven special things that accompany salvation and these are: 1. Knowledge . . . 2. Faith . . . 3. Repentance . . . 4. Obedience . . 5. Love . . . 6. Prayer . . . 7. Perseverance."[14]

He then elaborated how one might be assured of one's salvation by revealing:

---

[11] Adams, III:138.
[12] John Tillotson, *The Works of John Tillotson* (London: B. Aylmer, 1701), p. 97.
[13] Brooks, II:431.
[14] *Ibid.*

A sound and well-grounded assurance is attended with:
(1) a deep admiration of God's transcendent love and favor to the soul in the Lord Jesus . . .
(2) an earnest and an impatient longing after a further, a
clearer, and fuller enjoyment of God and Christ . . .
(3) a strong assault by Satan on all sides . . .
(4) making a man bold as a lion, valiant and gallant for
Christ and his cause, in the face of all dangers and
deaths . . .
(5) a desire to make others happy . . .
(6) an arming and strengthening against all wickedness
and baseness, Ezek. 16:60–63 . . .
(7) love, humility, holy joy . . .
(8) the testimony and witness of the Spirit of God. . .[15]

In another sermon more specifically dealing with one's
outward response to sin, the venerable Brooks wrote:

The infallible evidences of true saving faith are:
(1) A universal willingness to be rid of all sin;
(2) A constant, habitual willingness to be rid of all sin;
(3) A superlative willingness to be rid of all sin;
(4) A soul that does not indulge himself in a course of
sin, or in the common practice of any known sin, is
certainly a gracious soul.
(5) He that conflicts most with heart sins, and is most
affected with spiritual sins, and that laments and
mourns most over secret sins, invisible sins, sins that
be hid and remote from the eyes of the world, he
certainly is a gracious soul.[16]

One of the clearest works on the subject of assurance was
written by Anthony Burgess. In *Spiritual Refining: A Treatise
of Grace and Assurance*, Burgess saw two main hindrances to

---

[15] Brooks, II:512–18.
[16] Brooks, III:306–15.

assurance: self-love and carnal confidence, and temptation to unbelief by drawing false conclusions. Burgess also addressed the issue of identifying the difficulties to assurance. He stated two main causes:

> The difficulty of assurance arises from:
> 1. Our proneness to walk negligently and carelessly.
> 2. outward causes: a.) Satan—if he cannot hinder us in our duties, then he will hinder us in our comforts. b.) God—he makes assurance difficult that his favor may be more prized.[17]

Not wanting to leave the hearer in a depressed state, the Puritan mentor continued:

> What to do when we lack assurance:
> a.) Consider whether there be any allowance (not committing of) for sin;
> b.) See if you are careless or negligent in the means of grace;
> c.) Remember, God gives and lifts feelings of assurance;
> d.) Continue to obey God, though assurance may not be present. Thou art bound to love God, trust in him, perform all duties, though thy heart should never feel God's love to thee; for although the assurance of God's favor be like coals of fire poured upon the soul to melt it, yet we stand obligated to the spiritual exercise of holy duties, though God should never give us this encouragement.[18]

Since God was the author and the bestower of the grace of assurance, the Puritans spent great moments of thought pon-

---

[17] Anthony Burgess, *Spiritual Refining: A Treatise on Assurance* (London: A. Miller, 1652), p. 121.
[18] *Ibid*, p. 124.

dering why God in His mercy would be pleased to with-draw such a comfort or not give it to the converted for a sea-son. Again, Burgess wrote:

> Why does God not always give assurance to true
> Christians?
> a.) that we may taste and see how bitter sin is;
> b.) to keep us low and humble in ourselves; how excel-
> lent is it when others can behold and admire the graces
> of God in thee, yet thou apprehend none of these in thy
> own self.
> c.) so when we have assurance, we may more highly es-
> teem it, and the more prize it, taking greater heed not
> to lose it.
> d.) so we may demonstrate our obedience to him and
> give the greater honor to him. To rely upon God by
> faith, when thou hast no sensible testimonies of his love
> to thee, is the purest and meekest act of obedience that
> can be. Such faith of adherence did Christ put forth in
> his agonies. A man may desire assurance, as it breeds
> peace and ease to his soul, but to depend upon God in
> spiritual desertions, is wholly to give all to God and
> nothing to himself. The way of assurance brings more
> comfort to thyself, but the way of believing gives more
> glory to God.
> e.) so thou mayest be an experienced Christian able to
> comfort others in their distress. He that is not tempted
> about the pardon of sin, wonders at those who are so
> afflicted, and therefore is altogether unskillful to apply
> fit remedies.[19]

In concluding his powerful presentation of the full range of his teachings on assurance, Burgess gave these final instructions:

---

[19] *Ibid.*

How to get assurance:
a.) Give all diligence to obtaining it; he that never doubts will never learn.
b.) Fruitfully, fervently, and actively walk in all the ways of holiness.
c.) Exercise humility and meekness; avoid all presumptions and self-righteousness.
c.) Watch against all known sin.
e.) Take heed of grieving the Spirit of God, or quenching the motions of it.
f.) Acquaint thyself well with the Covenant of the gospel, with the precious promises revealed there, with the gracious condescension of God's love in Christ.[20]

The reason for such emphasis on practical holiness was that the Puritans knew that an unregenerate person could not attain the degree of holiness that would evidence a work of grace in the heart. They also knew that the regenerate could not perform any works pleasing to God apart from the grace given by God to accomplish such a work. Holiness was evidence of the presence of God. However, they did not ascribe to the doctrine of sinless perfection. These preachers knew the battle with sin that took place within the unregenerate members of the body; therefore, they knew there might be degrees of assurance. While they knew that "sin might rebel in a saint, but it shall never reign in a saint,"[21] the Puritan ministers were careful not to teach sinless perfection. Recognizing this possibility, Thomas Brooks stated:

You must never judge yourselves unsound or hypocrites by those things which the Scripture never makes a character of an unsound Christian, or of an hypocrite. Many a Christian has his pardon sealed in the court of

---

[20] Brooks, III:331.
[21] *Ibid.*

> heaven before it is sealed in the court of his own con-
> science. . . . Every breach of peace with God is not a
> breach of covenant with God. . . . They are not so apt to
> question the truth of their grace as those that are truly
> gracious.[22]

Assurance of saving faith was a ministry that only God could accomplish. Richard Sibbes's statement that "no less a person than God is needed to assure us of God's love"[23] formed the crux of the Puritan concept. Modern evangelism of the Finney type is much different in application of assurance because it is much different in its origin. Two basic assumptions prevail: assurance is a ministry that can be conferred upon a believer by another person; and assurance rests only upon Scripture promises. Law Four of "The Four Spiritual Laws" states that "we must individually receive Jesus Christ as Savior and Lord; then we can know and experience God's love and plan for our lives." Immediately after the person receives Christ by personal invitation, the user of the evangelical handpiece is instructed to take the new convert through a series of questions to ensure assurance of salvation. The basic question is, "How do you know that Christ is in your life?" The printed sequence of questions and answers to be given is as follows:

> Did you receive Christ into your life? According to His
> promise in Revelation 3:20, where is Christ right now
> in relation to you? Christ said that He would come into
> your life. Would He mislead you? On what authority do
> you know that God has answered your prayer? (The

---

[22] Brooks, III:299.

[23] John Blanchard, *Gathered Gold* (Hertfordshire, England: Evangelical Press, 1984), p. 8.

trustworthiness of God Himself and His Word.)[24]

While what the document states is true, the booklet has the potential to mislead people into an assurance because they agree with certain facts, even though they may not have been given a new heart. The Puritans made it very clear that there was a close relationship between assurance and obedience; much of modern evangelical teaching gives assurance to those who are at home in the realm of sin, and may perpetuate a damning hoax upon the naive or unknowing. The *Evangelism Explosion* manual features a typical conversation between a person sharing the gospel and a person who has just trusted Christ for his salvation. After taking the individual through several promise passages, one of which is John 6:47, the gospel presenter is trained to say something like this:

> "Who are you now trusting, Rene, for your salvation? Jesus Christ? He says, he that believeth, this is he that trusteth in Me—that doesn't mean an intellectual assent, for you have believed in Christ all your life. This doesn't mean trusting Him for temporal affairs. You've done that all your life. Saving faith means trusting Christ alone for eternal salvation. This is what you have done today. Jesus says that you have everlasting life. Do you believe Him?"
>
> "Yes, I do."
>
> "Rene, if you should die in your sleep tonight, where would you wake up?"

---

24 "The Four Spiritual Laws" (San Bernardino, Calif., Campus Crusade for Christ, Int., 1965).

"In heaven."

"God said it. That settles it. Praise the Lord! Welcome, Rene, to the family of God."[25]

As with "The Four Spiritual Laws," and other so-called tracts or witnessing tools, the assumption is made that a person sharing Christ can, and is expected to, pronounce assurance upon the new believer solely upon the basis of the convert's faith in the promises of a few verses. The Scofield Bible defines assurance as follows:

> Assurance is the believer's full conviction that, through the work of Christ alone, received by faith, he is in possession of a salvation in which he is eternally kept. And this assurance rests only upon the Scripture promises to him who believes.[26]

Modern Finneyism eliminates two of the three elements the Puritans vigorously held to that formed the basis of a well-grounded assurance: the witness of the Spirit and the conduct and character of the convert. Much modern teaching on assurance gives no credence to the Puritan contention that the Bible taught that, unless a convert gave diligent attention to one's spiritual growth in sanctification, there would be no complete grounds for assurance of that hope. The Puritans were equally careful in their instruction not to promote error on the opposite side by making holiness and obedience the ground of assurance instead of the work of Christ. They carefully taught that the Holy Spirit witnessed to Christ as

---

[25] D. James Kennedy, *Evangelism Explosion* (Wheaton: Tyndale, 1973), p. 55.
[26] The Scofield Bible (New York: Oxford Univ. Press, 1945), p. 1322.

the sole ground of one's peace and hope. To do otherwise would have been to commit an error of equally grievous proportions as does modern evangelism in promoting antinomianism.

Chapter 7

Conclusion

Puritan preaching was distinctly evangelical, but evangelical in a much different sense from what is offered today in main line evangelicalism. Puritan evangelism was as much of a theological system then as what is offered today. Both systems have salient features.

Comparisons

The three leading features of modern Finneyism are: an emphasis on instantaneous conversion; a system of invitation that includes the unconverted who wish to receive Christ being distinguished from those who don't by inviting the former to come to the front; the pronouncement of assurance of salvation immediately after trusting Christ based solely on scriptural promises.

The purpose of this work is not to debate the correctness of requiring an individual response to the proclamation of the gospel. Whenever preaching is relegated to the presentation of facts without any attempt to apply them to the conscience (leaving the impression that there is no divine command requiring true repentance and faith), biblical Christianity wilts away. An invariable characteristic of apostolic preaching has been the divinely bestowed assurance that the proclamation of the evangel is the divinely ordained means for the conviction and conversion of the unregenerate. Thus, an inherent expectation in evangelical preaching is that God may be pleased to use the foolishness of preaching to bring the responsive of heart to Himself. The question of whether it is right to invite men to Christ is indisputable to those who rest in God's Word. However, this discussion concerns another issue: namely, which of the two evangelical systems compares most closely in message content to the biblical pattern demonstrated in the Book of Acts.

The Puritan system, and indeed it may be considered a system because its message dictated its methodology, also had three prominent features. Doctrinally, Puritanism proclaimed a broad and vigorous Calvinism; experimentally, the system offered a warm and contagious devotional kind of Christianity; evangelistically, it heralded a tender, aggressive, and impassioned message of substitutionary satisfaction. While modern Finneyism stresses methodology, the system of Puritan evangelism stressed theology (see Appendix).

To fully appreciate Puritan preaching, one must be aware of the distinctives that rendered their preaching and writing so powerful. As a rule, these distinctives have been removed from modern exposition. Granted, there are several areas in which modern evangelism and Puritan evangelism agree, such as the free offer of the gospel and that salvation is found through the meritorious work of the Lord Jesus. However, Puritan preaching was marked by features which are in great contrast to modern preaching.

The first obvious distinctive of Puritan preaching was the message content. The preaching of the Puritans was a scriptural evangel. One will find numerous instances where as many as ten to fifteen biblical phrases may appear in one sentence. The Word of God can be found to be woven into the very thought patterns of these pastors. One may find quotations from the books of Moses, Obadiah, the apostles, and the Lord Jesus in the same sentence all supporting and strengthening one another. One would suspect that the Holy

Spirit had burned into the hearts of these men the very words of God. Of course here is where Puritan theology dictated Puritan methodology. The Puritans understood God to be the only one who could convince, convict, convert, and comfort the sinner through the Word. The task of His messengers, then, was to communicate that Word by teaching and applying it to the conscience. Preachers were to declare God's mind and heart as set forth in the passage chosen so that the Holy Spirit, who did not work in a vacuum, would use the revealed truth to enable a lost soul to come to Christ. Their message was their method.

Not only was the Puritan message scriptural, it was also doctrinal. They articulated doctrinal principles by distinguishing things that differed. When they talked about sin, they compared it to the glorious heaven that was ruled by a holy God. The hearer or reader knew what sin was after being exposed to such clear and well-defined terms. This doctrinal emphasis was woven into all their writings. One can clearly see the doctrines of the general call and the effectual call of God in the clucking of chickens in John Bunyan's masterpiece, *Pilgrim's Progress*. The Puritan evangel was steeped with clear doctrinal instruction.

In the matter of doctrine one may safely state that the Puritans were Calvinists, with their basic proposition being the biblical principle that "salvation is of the Lord" (Jonah 2:9). Thus, the Puritans emphasized the activity of the Triune God in salvation: election by the Father, redemption by the Son, and effectual calling by the Holy Spirit. To label them hyper-Calvinists is unfair, for these divines made a full and free offer of Christ to sinners and passionately urged the sinner to seek Him and settle with Christ.

Besides being scriptural and doctrinal, Puritan preaching was also symmetrical; that is, it contained the whole counsel of God. The Puritans were not squeamish in letting a passage say what it meant for fear of not getting a response from the audience. If the text said that salvation was a difficult and rare thing, that one must strive in one's quest to reach God, the Puritan would let it stand as written. On the other hand, if a text said that he who believes has life, they let that passage speak in all its freeness and gospel glory. The Puritans had a beautiful symmetry in the proclamation of the gospel. Much of modern preaching appears to be more concerned with acquainting the audience with one's past life and God's present blessing rather than scriptural and doctrinal truth. One of today's glaring errors in evangelistic preaching is the overemphasis on the simplicity of the gospel. The gospel has become something that one gets rather than something that God chooses to do for sinners flowing from a heart of grace and mercy. The sum of the gospel was defined by Thomas Manton:

> The sum of the gospel is this: that all those who by true repentance and faith do forsake the flesh, the world, and the devil, and give themselves up to God the Father, Son, and Holy Spirit as their creator, redeemer, and sanctifier shall find God as a Father, taking them for his reconciled children, and for Christ's sake pardoning their sin, and by his Spirit giving them his grace; and if they persevere in this course will finally glorify them and bestow upon them everlasting happiness; but will condemn the unbelievers impenitent and ungodly to everlasting punishment.[1]

That sum of the gospel is quite different from "trust Jesus to take you to heaven when you die." There is glorious

---

[1] Thomas Manton, *The Complete Works of Thomas Manton* (rpt. Worthington, Pa.: Maranatha Publications, n.d.), II:102–03.

symmetry in the Manton statement: repentance, faith, being returned to God (Father, Son, and Spirit), justified, sanctified and glorified at the end of a perseverance. That was the Puritan message—a beautiful scriptural, doctrinal, and symmetrical presentation of the work of God.

The second major distinctive of Puritan preaching was its foundation of biblical theism, the proper doctrine of God. The Puritans made no assumption that their audiences had any true knowledge of God at all; thus, they vigorously presented God in all His fullness as the basis of any message. God as Creator was involved in everything from the superintendence of their lives to the disposition of His common and sovereign graces. Puritan messages always began with God as their focus. The gospel was about God, from God, and for God; man was the beneficiary of what God as author, accomplisher, and applier of redemption was pleased to do.

Modern evangelism, especially in its literature, places man at the center. In a system which believes that man is the initiator and motivator of ministry instead of God, messages and tracts must be oriented to appeal to the individual. Granted, people do come to Christ through the use of such tools. There are truths contained in these handpieces and God will use whatever amount of truth is needed to draw a sinner to Himself. The subtlety, however, of a man-centered approach can be very damaging and deceptive. The following tract is exemplary of today's man-centered emphasis:

> Your Potential—Jesus came that you might have life and have it abundantly.
>
> Your Fall—But your sins (thinking wrong and doing wrong) have withheld good from you.
>
> Your Solution—For God so loved you that He gave His

only Son, that if you believe in Him, you will have ever-lasting life.

Your Choice—To all who receive Him, to those who believe He is, He gives the right to become children of God.

Your Prayer—"Dear God, I confess my sin; I have done wrong. I ask you to forgive me. Come into my life right now. Make me the person you intended me to be. Help me to love you and follow you the rest of my life. Thank you for hearing me and answering my prayer. I do trust you, God. I pray to you now through Jesus Christ my Savior. Amen."

Unlock all of your potential. It affects your whole life.[2]

Man is the focus of today's evangelism; God was the focus of Puritan evangelism. The doctrinally watered-down man-centered gospel of neo-Finneyism often fails to evoke deep reverence, deep repentance, and deep humility, as well as a spirit of worship or concern for the local church. In general, modern evangelism does not produce theocentric converts.

The Puritans, as another distinctive, were not afraid to use the law of God as an instrument of evangelism. The Puritans believed that God called people in different ways. Some he called in a sovereign gospel way, like Saul of Tarsus. To this persecutor of the church, God demonstrated His eternal purposes in the salvation of this rebel by calling him on the road to Damascus. Even when Paul wrote about it himself, he stated that his calling came "when it pleased God" (Gal. 1:15–16). The Puritans understood that salvation

---

[2] *Enjoying Life* (Silver Spring, Md.: Great Commissions, Inc., 1984).

was a matter of God's timing when God chose to reveal His
Son to a sinner for His glory and purpose. They also knew
that some God called from the womb, such as John the
Baptist. Some they knew were called on the hour of death,
such as the thief on the cross—so that none may despair, but
only one example so that none may presume. The fourth
way, which was to the Puritans the most common way, was
by a prior working of the law in the heart. They regarded the
law in its killing, slaying work as the right proclamation and
application of the gospel.[3]

   To be honest in this evaluation, we must admit that some
of the Puritans carried this prior law work to the point of ex-
treme, demanding unbiblical steps and evidences of deep-
seated conviction necessary to conversion. However, as a
general statement, this author can say that the majority of the
Puritans had a good understanding of the application of the
law in terms of preparing the sinner to be heartily sensible to
one's guilt before God. The Puritans preached that unless a
person was affected by this conviction, all the provisions of
gospel grace would be slighted. They used the law to show
men that God stood as an angry judge and in His wrath
burned toward the sinner, His claims and throne rights
having been denied, His laws spurned; hence sinful man
stood under His wrath and condemnation.[4] These preachers
of law and grace sought to convince man that he had a twofold problem: that of a bad record (a legal problem), and that
of a bad heart (a moral problem), both of which made one
unfit for the presence of God. By revealing the one problem

---

[3] William Guthrie, *The Christian's Great Interest* (1658; rpt. Carlisle, Pa.:
Banner of Truth, 1969), pp. 37–53.

[4] Jonathan Edwards, *The Complete Works of Jonathan Edwards* (Carlisle,
Pa.: Banner of Truth, 1979), II:712.

they sought to bring sinners to a sense of their condemnation, the bad record; by the other to a place of despair in light of their depravity, the bad heart.[5]

The preaching of today's evangel is generally confined to communicating to the sinner that one has a little legal problem and that, as a result of the bad things one has done, one is separated from God.[6] But the Puritans realized that Jesus Christ was a Savior not only from what one had done, but also from what one was. They knew a sinner would never lay hold of the righteousness of Christ for what one had done that was wrong until one realized that the labors of one's hands could not fulfill God's demands; so no sinner would lay hold of an omnipotent Christ to change him in terms of what one was, until one could say, "Foul and full of sin I am."[7] Christ was a Savior from both; as a result, there was no division of justification and sanctification which is the theological root behind such deeper-life movements as the Keswick Movement. Whenever the gospel is presented in terms of having dealt with only the legal issue and Christ only as a Savior from legal guilt, one must now deal with the person who says his legal problem has been cured but is still living in full expression of the corruption that he is. The Puritans did not have that problem because the gospel they preached secured not only the justification, but also the sanctification of the sinner.

Fourth, Puritan preaching was marked by a discriminating application of truth. One cannot read long in Puritan literature without being struck with the keenness with which

---

[5] Joseph Alleine, *An Alarm to the Unconverted*, (1671; rpt. Carlisle, Pa.: Banner of Truth, 1978), pp. 50–68.

[6] "The Four Spiritual Laws," (Campus Crusade For Christ, Inc., 1965).

[7] Edwards, II:7–12.

they searched out the differences in their hearers and sought to apply the truth to them in their specific categories. Before ever addressing what true conversion was, Joseph Alleine spent pages presenting what conversion was not. In lucid detail, Pastor Alleine presented ten marks of the unconverted man. Then, perhaps in an effort not to miss anyone in his reading audience, Alleine then revealed twelve marks of an unregenerate heart.[8] The Puritans were masters in distinguishing between true and false conversion, true and false believers, and true and false assurance. As wise surgeons, they sought to apply the truth to their flocks in order to prescribe the right medicine for the right malady.

Much of modern preaching invites people "to come to Christ just as you are." Only in a few instances and in a few articles are sinners instructed as to why they should come to Christ, and what they are to come for, and from whence they have come. Christ is often relegated to a band-aid rather than a heart surgeon.

The fifth Puritan distinctive is really an outgrowth of their penchant for truthful application. They taught a well-grounded doctrine of assurance. Volumes are written on this subject alone. Perhaps the clearest and most profound would be Jonathan Edwards's *Treatise on Religious Affections.* The entire purpose of the treatise is to distinguish between true and false conversion. As presented earlier, the Puritans preached an assurance based upon the promises of God in the work of salvation, the inner confirmation by the Spirit of God, and the revealed character and conduct of the converted. The Puritans preached an assurance based upon holding up the standard of Scripture which described a true believer. Then, they instructed their hearers to be as honest and ob-

---

[8] Alleine, p. 45.

jective as one would have to be on the day of judgment, and answer the question of whether or not one was what the Scripture said a Christian was. At this point, this writer again will admit that many Puritans went too far in making fine distinctions which troubled the conscience of the sensitive and were totally unheeded by the indifferent. But if the Puritans went too far in this direction, modern evangelism has fallen far short.

Modern instruction on assurance is ignorant and inconsistent to say the least. To hold exclusively to the first element of what the Puritans taught without the second and third is Antinomianism. To hold exclusively to the second without the first and third is either hypocrisy or the deepest self-delusion or fantasy. Many modern converts, when asked how they know they are saved, respond by saying, "My heart tells me I am." When pressed to explain on what basis such a claim can be made, a typical response might be, "Because my heart tells me that it is." In other words, they are saying that "I must be saved because I know that I'm saved." The Puritans would say that the grounds of assurance are not to be found in the heart alone, but in the standard upheld by the Word. To hold exclusively, however, to the third without the first and the second is legalism. Clearly, much of modern preaching teaches that assurance is a ministry that man can perform; the Puritans held that it was a grace that only God could give by confirming through His Word, through His Spirit, and by the evidence of perfecting grace in the life of the converted.

Distinctive number six is that the Puritans preached the whole Christ to the whole man. The concept of Christ being offered as a prophet, priest, and king was a hallmark of biblical preaching in the Puritan era. Therefore, one observes no attempt on the part of the Puritan divines to offer Christ as a savior from the penalty of sin while deliberately ignoring His claims as a sovereign and a Lord and His demands that one forsake the love and practice of sin. Apparently the tendency to separate the offices and the benefits of Christ was common during their age, for Alleine stated:

> All of Christ is accepted by the sincere convert. He loves not only the wages but the work of Christ, not only the benefits but the burden of Christ. He is willing not only to tread out the corn, but to draw under the yoke. He takes up the commands of Christ, yes, the cross of Christ.
>
> The unsound convert takes Christ by halves. He is all for the salvation of Christ, but he is not for sanctification. He is for the privileges, but does not appropriate the person of Christ. He divides the offices and the benefits of Christ. This is an error in the foundation. Whoever loves life, let him beware here. It is an undoing mistake, of which you have been often warned, and yet none is more common.[9]

The Puritans preached a dominion of Christ as well as the deliverance by Christ. The tendency in today's evangelism is to offer Christ as Savior to the unconverted, and, should increasing righteousness not prevail as the bent of the supposed believer's life, then to justify or assure the professor of salvation under the guise of not yet having made Him Lord. In a system that is based upon man making the difference, evangelical evaluation must be by numbers, by bigness rather than by quality, in order to justify the ministry of the evangelist, and to garner financial support. Not so with the

---

[9] Alleine, p. 46.

serious-minded Puritans. Alleine continued his diatribe against such a separation of Christ as Savior and Christ as Lord:

> They [the unsound converts] will not have Him as God offers, "to be a Prince and a Saviour" (Acts v.31). They divide what God has joined, the King and the Priest. They will not accept the salvation of Christ as He intends it; they divide it here. Every man's vote is for salvation from suffering, but they do not desire to be saved from sinning. They would have their lives saved, but still would have their lusts. Indeed, many divide here again. . . . The sound convert takes a whole Christ, and takes Him for all intents and purposes, without exceptions, without limitations, without reserve. He is willing to have Christ upon any terms.[10]

The seventh distinction was the clarion call to repentance. The Puritans believed that if the gospel was preached and did not sound a certain note, then no one would know what to follow. That certain note was repentance; the only way to settle the Son question was to deal with the sin question. Alleine stated that "the objects from which we turn in conversion are sin, Satan, the world, and our own righteousness."[11] The theology of the Puritans affected their message greatly at this point. They believed Acts 5:31, "He is the one whom God exalted to His right hand as a Prince and a Savior, to grant repentance to Israel and forgiveness of sins." They knew that one of the works of the risen Christ, and only the omnipotent Christ could do it, was to take the sinner who loved his sin, who drank iniquity like water, who was wedded to his lusts, and bring him to the place where he was not

---

[10] *Ibid*, p. 46.
[11] *Ibid*, p. 37.

only no longer reluctant but glad to forsake the darling bosom sins of his heart, and to turn to God with a full resolve to honor Him and obey Him and to make Him his end. They knew that only the mighty ascended Christ could perform such a work. Thus, their theology demanded that they preach a biblical standard of conversion with a clear note of repentance, for they knew that only God could bring man to submit on those terms and that God would bring an innumerable multitude to Himself on those terms, and on no lesser terms.[12]

The soft-pedaling of the biblical doctrine of repentance is inseparably linked to a denial of the truth that salvation is of God. If man is taught that he contributes to his salvation, then he must also be taught that there are demands that he can meet without the aid of the Holy Spirit. Such is much of modern evangelistic preaching. Modern-day techniques of leading someone to Christ either omit or hardly mention repentance.[13] Not so with the Puritans; they preached repentance and faith, not with the embellishments of an orchestral arrangement, but with the simplicity of a trumpet—turn or burn.

Another area that is distinctly Puritan was their concept of the magnitude of the work of conversion. The Puritans did not believe that true conversion was ordinarily the work of a moment, performed in an atmosphere of giddiness and lightness by one whose mind had not been brought to the place of deep sobriety and serious thought concerning the great issues of sin and eternity. Richard Baxter wrote:

---

12 *Ibid*, pp. 30–49.
13 The so-called "Roman Road" series of verses: Rom. 3:23; Rom. 6:23; Rom. 5:8; Rom. 10:9; Rom. 10:13.

Oh, sirs, conversion is another kind of work than most are aware of. It is no small matter to bring an earthly mind to heaven, and to show man the amiable excellencies of God till he be taken up in such love to him that can never be quenched; to break the heart for sin and to make him flee for refuge to Christ and thankfully embrace him as the life of his soul; to have the very drift and bent of his life changed so that a man renounces that which he took for his happiness, and places his happiness where he never did before, and lives not to the same end, drives not in the same design in the world as he formerly did; in a word, he that is in Christ is a new creature.[14]

Again from the pen of Joseph Alleine:

Never think you can convert yourself. If ever you would be savingly converted, you must despair of doing it in your own strength. It is a resurrection from the dead (Eph. ii.1) a new creation (Gal. vi.15; Eph. ii.10), a work of absolute omnipotence (Eph. i.19). Are not these out of the reach of human power? If you have not more than you had by your first birth, a good nature, a meek and chaste temper, etc., you are a stranger to true conversion. This is a supernatural work.[15]

The last distinctive of Puritan preaching uncovered by this project was the distinctive of not usurping the office of the Holy Spirit. The Puritans knew that whether it was when the saints gathered to worship or when they proclaimed the evangel of God, if almighty God did not do something, nothing would happen. They knew that unless

---

[14] Richard Baxter, *The Practical Works of Richard Baxter* (Ligonier, Pa.: 1991), IV:8–9.
[15] Alleine, pp. 26–27.

God broke out of heaven and opened blind eyes and un-
stopped the deaf ears, they would be a miserable failure and
a flop. At the very beginning of his tract to the unconverted,
the Puritan evangelist, Alleine, penned these words:

> But, O Lord, how insufficient I am for this work. Alas,
> with what shall I pierce the scales of Leviathan, or make
> the heart feel that is hard as the nether millstone? Shall
> I go speak to the grave, and expect the dead will obey
> me and come forth? Shall I make an oration to the
> rocks, or declaim to the mountains, and think to move
> them with arguments? Shall I make the blind to see?
> From the beginning of the world was it not heard that a
> man opened the eyes of the blind (John ix.32)? But, O
> Lord, Thou canst pierce the heart of the sinner. . . . I
> can only draw the bow at a venture but do Thou direct
> the arrow between the joints of the harness. Slay the
> sin, and save the soul of the sinner that casts his eyes on
> these pages.[16]

One of the sad earmarks of modern evangelism, which
includes preaching, personal witnessing, and evangelistic
tracts and training books, is a continued attempt to have everything so arranged that if God the Holy Spirit did not come
within miles of the event, one would still have something to
show for what was done. This mindset comes directly from
Charles Finney.[17] The history of American evangelism is
displayed in meticulous detail at the Billy Graham Center
for Evangelism located on the campus of Wheaton College in

---

[16] Alleine, pp. 15–16.
[17] Charles G. Finney, *Revival Lectures* (Broadview, Il.: Cicero Bible
Press, n.d.), Chapter II, "When A Revival Is To Be Expected";
Chapter III, "How to Promote a Revival"; Chapter XIV, "Measures to
Promote Revival."

Wheaton, Illinois. On the wall is a plaque revealing the concept of revival as taught by Finney. The plaque reads:

> A revival of religion is not a miracle. It is not a miracle, or dependent on a miracle, in any sense . . . a revival is the result of the right use of the appropriate means.

From that point on in history, evangelism took a dramatic shift, moving away from seeing revival as a God-centered, sovereignly ordained visitation of God in all His power to the highly organized and scheduled revivalism of today. Modern evangelism has perfected the mindset of Finney. Mass evangelism as well as personal sharing of the gospel carries with it the mindset that what one does makes a difference; therefore, one must do everything correctly and in order. Puritan preaching did not usurp the office and ministry of God the Spirit in either the proclamation of the gospel or in the application of the message to an individual.

The defects of a theological system with such a man-centered focus as the one contrasted with the Puritan system pose great concerns. This writer's concerns would be these: (1) Instantaneous conversion should be pressed home, but not in such a way that conveys the idea that unless one is powerfully converted to God immediately one is not converted at all. This emphasis forces the converting work of the Holy Spirit to be of a single fashion and far too narrow in application. It also places the emphasis upon man, both as the agent who brings about the conversion ("I led him to Christ") and as the one who decides to be saved. (2) People should be instructed to come to Christ "just as you are," but not at the expense of proper instruction about the holiness of God's law, the depth of one's sinfulness, and the guilt and cause of sin. To tell an individual that one needs to come to

Christ is of little use, unless one is told why one needs to come and from what one needs to come. Also, sinners must be taught clearly what is saving faith. Faith not properly explained is faith that is mere feeling. If faith is explained only as believing that Christ died for sinners, then the demons have faith. (3) To insist that all new believers experience immediate assurance of their salvation is most unsafe. Assurance is not of the essence of saving faith; there may be saving faith without assurance. By telling a new convert that one may know the assurance of one's salvation on the basis of what one has done is to manufacture assured converts at man's pleasure. The sovereignty of God in saving and confirming that work on biblical grounds is removed and may lead to eternal deception. The professed convert may never pass the test to see if one is in the faith, and believing in spite of biblical evidence to the contrary may cause one to cease seeking the Savior.

Such a man-centered system could do incalculable damage to the souls of men. After comparing the two systems of evangelism, this author is convinced that a common confusion exists in the proponents of modern evangelism based upon Finney's new measures. The gospel of God does call for an immediate response from all who hear; but it does not require the same response from all who hear. The immediate duty of the unprepared sinner is not to try to believe on Christ, which he is unable to do because of sin. One must read, inquire and use the means of grace to learn from what he needs to be saved. An unregenerate person does not have the ability to accept Christ at any moment, as Finney supposed.

If a pastor tells his flock that they are under obligation to receive Christ at any moment and demands in God's name that they decide for Christ at once, some who are spiritually unprepared will try to do so; they will come forward and accept directions and "go through the motions" and go away thinking they have received Christ. But they may not actually have received Christ because they were not able to do so. So a crop of false conversions is likely to be produced in the name of Christ by the nature of the system and methodology of evangelism employed, as indicated by the statistics in Chapter 1. While many in our country profess to have been saved, the true fruits of repentance are not observed in their lives as a result of a true work of grace on the part of God. Modern evangelism tends to try to bring the work of the Holy Spirit to a precipitate conclusion, to pick the fruit before it is ripe. The result is false conversions, hypocrisy, and hardening of hearts. The appeal for immediate decisions presupposes that men are free to decide for Christ at any time. The basis of such a hypothesis is a disastrous view of sin.

What, then, are some principles that should govern modern preaching as gleaned from this comparison of the two historical systems of evangelism?

Uses

1. At the outset, as the Puritans would insist, one must understand that evangelistic preaching is not a special kind of preaching with its own distinctive style. Preaching of this sort must be part of the ordinary public ministry of the Word. This means that the guidelines which govern evangelistic preaching are the same guidelines that govern all public preaching of God's Word. This would also mean that the primary, but by all means not the only, person charged with the task of evangelistic preaching is the local pastor. John Owen, referring to pastors, stated that "it is his duty in the course of his public and private ministry of the Word,

diligently to labour for the conversion of souls to God."[18] J. I. Packer described the pastor's ministry with the following charge:

> What God requires of him is that he should be faithful to the content of the gospel, and diligent in imparting it. He is to seek by all public means to make his sermon clear, memorable, and relevant to the lives of his hearers; he is to pray earnestly for God's blessing on his preaching, that it may be "in the demonstration of the Spirit and of power"; but it is not part of his business to study to "dress up" the gospel and make it "appeal" to the natural man. The preacher's calling is very different from that of the commercial traveller, and the "quick sale" technique has no place in the Christian pulpit. The preacher is not sent of God to make a quick sale, but to deliver a message. When he has done that, his work in the pulpit is over. It is not his business to try and exhort "decisions." It is God's own sovereign prerogative to make His Word effective.[19]

One's theology is proved by one's methodology; therefore, the preacher's behavior must be governed by his recognition of, and subjection to, Divine sovereignty in his preaching. This would also include exhibiting that quiet confidence in evangelistic preaching as in all preaching as modeled by the Puritans. They were in no feverish panic about success because they knew God's Word would not return void; that God would use the foolishness of their preaching to call out His elect from all nations, not as a result of their preaching gifts and ingenuity, but by reason of God's sovereign operation. This was the mindset and spirit that

---

[18] J. I. Packer, "Puritan Evangelism," *The Banner of Truth* (n.d.), p. 12.
[19] *Ibid.*

God honored in Richard Baxter's Kidderminster ministry. For seventeen years, Baxter used no other means but sermons twice a week and catechetical instruction from house to house. Well over six hundred converts were brought to God, of whom Baxter wrote, six years after his ejection, "that, despite constant exposure to ridicule and obloquy for their Puritanism, not one that I know of has fallen from his sincerity."[20]

2. Ministers must preach the biblical gospel. The terms of the gospel are simple but not shallow; thus, all the counsel of God must be taught in scriptural proportion. Two or three of the more popular doctrines of the gospel must not be allowed to overshadow all other truths. True evangelical repentance as well as the true nature of sin must be a regular part of preaching. True saving faith, not easy believism must be heralded from the modern pulpit. God must become the focus of all preaching, not man. Man must be taught that God is the reason why God does everything; man is the recipient of what God purposes to do in the deep counsels of His own will (Isaiah 43:25, 48:9).

3. Ministers must make adequate room for the varied ministries of the Holy Spirit in preaching. Ministers cannot make a person a believer nor cause him to act like a believer; preachers cannot convince anyone of salvation. God must awaken before man will listen. Pastors must speak and let the Spirit arouse. The various works of the Spirit of God must be honestly stated and admitted; while instantaneous conversion is pressed on all men, it must not be taught as a necessity.

4. Ministers must put before people the true evidences of

---

20 Richard Baxter, *The Reformed Pastor* (1656; rept. Carlisle, Pa.: Banner of Truth, 1979), pp. 10–19.

saving faith. Those who profess Christ must be plainly warned to try themselves well according to the biblical standard. They must be instructed clearly that faith is not feeling, and that patient continuance in well-doing is the great proof of saving faith. Converts must be warned that the truly saved cannot sin successfully.

5. Ministers must preach the great duty of counting the cost. Pastors must constantly urge upon those who profess saving faith that there is warfare as well as peace, a cross as well as a crown in the service of Christ. The present ministry of the reigning Christ must be heralded to the people to ensure hope in the midst of battle, and reward as the fruit of peace. Christ's example of not flattering or encouraging volunteers to follow Him, but rather to stand still and count the cost (Luke 14:25), must govern one's shepherding from the pulpit.

6. Ministers must instruct their people in the practical use of divine truth. Present-day pastors must learn that their greatest counseling ministry must take place from the pulpit. Flocks must be taught to become doers of the word, not just hearers.

7. Ministers must guard and care for their own evangelical zeal. Pastors must always remember where they came from, that grace at flood stage swept them off their feet to be carried along by the Spirit of God to proclaim the saving gospel of King Jesus. Pastors must recognize that they must be a herald of truth while being a recipient of mercy. We must remember that ministry is not the result of human achievement, but of divine mercy (2 Cor. 4:1). Ministers must evaluate themselves not on popularity, but on faithfulness; not by "Does it work? but "Is it true?"

I am convinced that ministers of this age must sound the clarion call of the biblical gospel. I am convicted that this is what God wants to do in this generation, much as He did during the stressful days of our Puritan counterparts. But I also believe that He will do it in the same order that He has been pleased to use before: by giving pastors a heart that burns for sinners, eyes that are filled and spill down with tears for sinners, and gearing them to a clarion call of truth upon which He has put His seal to save sinners. Otherwise, all our man-centered efforts will be abortive. Just as preaching a God-owned message without a God-broken heart will be abortive, so to have the tearful heart without the God-focused message of the Puritans will fall short of that which God will do for His glory.

Bibliography

Adams, Thomas. *The Works of Thomas Adams*. 3 vols. 1630; rpt. Edinburgh: James Nichols, 1862.

Alleine, Joseph. *An Alarm to the Unconverted*. 1671; Rpt. 5th ed. Carlisle, Pa.: Banner of Truth, 1978.

Baxter, Richard. *The Practical Works of Richard Baxter*. 4 vols. Ligonier, Pa.: Soli Deo Gloria, 1990–91.

————*The Reformed Pastor*. 1656; Rpt. 5th ed. Carlisle, Pa.: Banner of Truth, 1979.

Blanchard, John, comp. ed. *Gathered Gold*. Hertfordshire, England: Evangelical Press, 1984.

Bolton, Samuel. *The True Bounds of Christian Freedom*. 1645; Rpt. Carlisle, Pa.: Banner of Truth, 1978.

Bonar, Horatius. *Words to the Winners of Souls*. 1950; Rpt. 2nd ed. Grand Rapids: Baker, 1981.

Booth, Abraham. *The Reign of Grace*. 1734; Rpt. Swengel, Pa.: Reiner Publications, 1976.

Boston, Thomas. *The Beauties of Boston*. 1831; Rpt. Inverness, Scotland: Christian Focus Publications, 1979.

————*The Complete Works of Thomas Boston*. 12 vols. Wheaton: Richard Owen Roberts, 1980.

Bradford, John. *The Works of John Bradford*. 2 vols. 1853; Rpt. Carlisle, Pa.: Banner of Truth, 1979.

Bridge, William. *A Lifting Up for the Downcast*. 1649; Rpt. Carlisle, Pa.: Banner of Truth, 1979.

Brooks, Thomas. *The Complete Works of Thomas Brooks*, 1862. Rpt. Carlisle, Pa.: Banner of Truth, 1980.

Burgess, Anthony. *Spiritual Refining: A Treatise on Assurance*. London: A. Miller, 1652.

Burroughs, Jeremiah. *The Excellency of A Gracious Spirit*. London: George Dawson, 1649 (This book has been reprinted by Soli Deo Gloria in a modern format).

———*Gospel Worship*. London: John Rothwell, 1648 (This book has been reprinted by Soli Deo Gloria in a modern format).

———*The Rare Jewel of Christian Contentment*. 1648; Rpt. Carlisle, Pa.: Banner of Truth, 1978.

Charnock, Stephen. *Discourses Upon the Existence and Attributes of God*. 1853; Rpt. 3rd ed. Grand Rapids: Baker, 1981.

Cradock, Samuel. *Knowledge and Practice*. London: William Grantham, 1673.

Dallimore, Arnold A. *George Whitefield*. 2 vols. Wheaton: Cornerstone Books, 1979.

Edwards, Jonathan. *The Complete Works of Jonathan Edwards*, rev. ed. Edward Hickman. 2 vols. Rpt. Carlisle, Pa.: Banner of Truth, 1979.

Finney, Charles G. *Autobiography*. Broadview, Il.: Cicero Bible Press, n.d.

———*Revival Lectures*. Broadview, Il.: Cicero Bible Press, n.d.

Flavel, John. *The Works of John Flavel*. 6 vols. 2nd ed. Carlisle, Pa.: Banner of Truth, 1982.

Flood, Robert. "What the Gallup Poll Says to Evangelicals," *Moody Monthly*, August 1980, pp. 22–27.

Ford, Leighton. *The Christian Persuader*. New York: Macmillan, 1966.

Gerstner, John H. *Jonathan Edwards, Evangelist*. Rpt. Pittsburgh: Soli Deo Gloria, 1996.

Gill, John. *A Body of Divinity*. 1890; Rpt. Grand Rapids: Sovereign Grace Books, 1971.

Goodwin, Thomas. *The Complete Works of Thomas Goodwin*. 12 vols. Edinburgh: James Nichols, 1863–65.

Gouge, William. *The Whole Armour of God*. London: John Beale, 1619.

Guthrie, William. *The Christian's Great Interest*. 1658; rpt. Carlisle, Pa.: Banner of Truth, 1969.

Hooker, Thomas. *The Poor Doubting Christian Drawn to Christ.* 1845; Rpt. Worthington, Pa.: Maranatha Publications, n.d.

Hopkins, Ezekiel. *The Works of Ezekiel Hopkins.* London: Jonathan Robinson, 1701.

Kennedy, D. James. *Evangelism Explosion.* 1970; Wheaton: Tyndale, 1973.

Lectures on Revival by the Ministers of Scotland. 1840; Rpt. Wheaton: Richard Owen Roberts, 1980.

Leighton, Robert. *The Whole Works of Robert Leighton,* Ed. John Norman Pearson. New York: J. C. Riker, 1853.

Love, Christopher. *The Combat Between the Flesh and the Spirit.* London: Thomas Cole, 1656 (This book has been reprinted by Soli Deo Gloria in a modern format).

Luther, Martin. *The Bondage of the Will.* Trans. Henry Cole. Rpt. 4th ed. Grand Rapids: Baker, 1981.

MacFarlan, D. *The Revivals of the Eighteenth Century.* 1847; Rpt. Wheaton: Richard Owen Roberts, 1980.

Manton, Thomas. *The Complete Works of Thomas Manton.* Rpt. Worthington, Pa.: Maranatha Publications, n.d.

Murray, Iain. *The Invitation System.* 2nd ed. Carlisle, Pa.: Banner of Truth, 1973.

Newton, John. *The Works of John Newton.* New York: Robert Carter and Brothers, 1856.

Nichols, James. *Puritan Sermons 1659–1689*. 6 vols Rpt. Wheaton: Richard Owen Roberts, 1981.

Owen, John. *The Death of Death in the Death of Christ*. Rpt. 3rd ed. Carlisle, Pa.: Banner of Truth, 1983.

————*The Works of John Owen*. Ed. William H. Goold. 16 vols. Rpt. 3rd ed. Carlisle, Pa.: Banner of Truth, 1977.

Packer, J. I. "Puritan Evangelism." *The Banner of Truth*.

Perkins, William. *The Works of William Perkins*. London: John Legatt, 1603.

Reisinger, Ernest C. *Today's Evangelism*. Phillipsburg, N. J.: Craig Press, 1982.

Roberts, Emyr, and R. Geraint Gruffydd. *Revival and Its Fruit*. Bryntirion, Wales: Evangelical Library of Wales, 1981.

Seed, Jeremiah. *Discourses on Several Important Subjects*. Vol. II. London: Manby and Cox, 1757.

Sermons of the Great Ejection. Rpt. London: Banner of Truth, 1962.

Shuffelton, Frank. *Thomas Hooker 1586–1647*. Princeton: Princeton University Press, 1977.

Sibbes, Richard. *The Works of Richard Sibbes*, ed. Alexander B. Grosart. 7 vols. Rpt. Carlisle, Pa.: Banner of Truth, 1973–1981.

Smith, Henry. *Works*. London: n.p., 1610.

Sprague, W. B. *Lectures on Revivals*. 1832; Rpt. 3rd ed. Carlisle, Pa.: Banner of Truth, 1978.

Spurgeon, Charles H. *An All Round Ministry*. Rpt. 3rd ed. Carlisle, Pa.: Banner of Truth, 1978.

————*Lectures to My Students*. 9th ed. Grand Rapids: Zondervan, 1970.

————*The New Park Street Pulpit and Metropolitan Tabernacle Pulpit Sermons, 1855–1917*; 63 vols. Rpt. Pasadena, Tex.: Pilgrim Publications, 1981.

————*The Soul Winner*. Rpt. Grand Rapids: Eerdmans, 1978.

Stanford, A. Ray. *Handbook of Personal Evangelism*. Florida Bible College, n.d.

Thomas, I. D. E., comp. ed. *The Golden Treasury of Puritan Quotations*. Carlisle, Pa.: Banner of Truth, 1977.

Tillotson, John. *The Works of John Tillotson*. London: B. Aylmer, 1701.

Tracy, Joseph. *The Great Awakening: A History of the Revival of Religion in the Time of Edwards and Whitefield*. Rpt. Carlisle, Pa.: Banner of Truth, 1976.

Traill, Robert. *The Works of Robert Traill*. 1810; Rpt. 4 vols. Carlisle, Pa.: Banner of Truth, 1975.

Tyler, Bennet. *New England Revivals*. 1846; Rpt. Wheaton: Richard Owen Roberts, 1980.

Watson, Thomas. *Body of Divinity*. 1890; Rpt. Grand Rapids: Baker, 1979.

Whitefield, George. *The Dairyman's Daughter and Other Personal Testimonies*. Rpt. Grand Rapids: Sovereign Grace Publishers, 1971.

Wright, Eric. *Tell the World*. Hertfordshire, England: Evangelical Press, 1981.

Additional Resources

Soli Deo Gloria has published the following titles on the subject of the Puritans and their ministry:

Brook, Benjamin. *Lives of the Puritans*
hardback, 3 volumes

Davies, Horton. *The Worship of the English Puritans*
paperback, 300 pages

Kevan, Ernest. *The Grace of Law:*
A Study in Puritan Theology, paperback, 300 pages

Kistler, Don. *A Spectacle Unto God:*
The Life and Death of Christopher Love.
hardback, 200 pages

Lewis, Peter. *The Genius of Puritanism*
paperback, 150 pages

Additionally, Soli Deo Gloria has reprinted the following titles referred to in the present work:

Burroughs, Jeremiah. *Gospel Worship.*
hardback, 360 pages

The Excellency of A Gracious Spirit
hardback, 260 pages

Gerstner, John H. *Jonathan Edwards, Evangelist*
paperback, 192 pages

Hopkins, Ezekiel. *The Works of Ezekiel Hopkins*
    hardback, 3 volumes

Love, Christopher. *The Combat Between the Flesh and the Spirit*
    hardback, 720 pages (contained in Volume 1 of
    The Works of Christopher Love)

Appendix

A Comparative Overview of the Plan of Salvation

The following chart depicts the contrast in the plan of salvation between modern Finneyism and Puritan evangelism, based upon the different theological views of God, the person and work of Christ, repentance and faith, and the response to the gospel. The characteristics of modern Finneyism are evident to various degrees in different circles of modern evangelism, and may not always be totally inclusive. However, they do represent the trends, directions, emphases, and mindset of current evangelism based upon the theology of the message which is communicated. The current methodology of evangelism is based upon these characteristics, just as the methodology of the Puritans was an outgrowth of their message.

Modern Finneyism	*Puritan Evangelism*
1. The view of the salvation process is determined by the needs of man.	1. The view of the salvation process is determined by the character of God.
2. Salvation emphasizes what man can receive from God.	2. Salvation emphasizes what God chose to accomplish for man.
3. The theme of salvation is the reception of eternal life.	3. The theme of salvation is the glory of God.
4. Man is the subject of salvation.	4. God is the subject of salvation.
5. There are varying degrees of man's ability to choose God.	5. Man is totally unable to choose God.
6. The Holy Spirit's role is to persuade.	6. The Holy Spirit's role is to apply.
7. The preacher's role is to preach for decisions—to battle the hearer's will.	7. The preacher's role is to preach to the conscience—to reveal truth.
8. The gospel is the offer of the possibility of salvation.	8. The gospel is the offer of the Savior.
9. The gospel emphasis is to meet the needs of man.	9. The gospel emphasis is to take people into the presence of God.
10. The central feature is the offer of eternal life.	10. The central feature is the offer of reconciliation, of which eternal life is a consequence.

11. Man is the reason why Christ died.

11. God is the reason why Christ died.

12. Man has the power to accept the gospel.

12. Man must be prepared by God to accept the gospel.

13. Evangelists fix the time for decision.

13. God determines the time for response.

14. Man can choose God at any time.

14. God causes man to choose at His time.

15. Assurance is a ministry assigned to man.

15. Assurance is a ministry assigned to the Holy Spirit.

16. Assurance is pronounced by man.

16. Assurance is affirmed by God and His Word.

17. The basis of assurance is scriptural promises.

17. The basis of assurance is scriptural promises, the inner work of the Spirit, and the character and conduct of the convert.

18. There is a relationship between faith and assurance.

18. There is a relationship between assurance, faith, and obedience.

19. The gospel secures justification.

19. The gospel secures justification and sanctification.

20. The gospel is something one gets.

20. The gospel is something God chooses to do.

21. The gospel is simple.

21. The gospel is simple, but not shallow.

22. The gospel is about man, from God, and for man.

22. The gospel is about God, from God, and for God.

23. The gospel deals with man's legal problem—sin.

24. Christ is a Savior from what one has done.

25. The offices and benefits of Christ are often separated.

23. The gospel deals with man's legal problem—sin—and man's moral problem—the heart.

24. Christ is a Savior from what one has done as well as what one is.

25. The offices and benefits of Christ are always combined.